MULTIPLICATION
DIVISION
WORKBOOK

 GRADE 3-4

THIS BOOK BELONGS TO:

TABLE OF CONTENTS

PART 1:

MULTIPLICATION PRACTICE

Multiplication Timed Tests (Tables 0 To 12)

Let's Multiply 0 & 1

1) $8 \times 0 = \boxed{}$ 2) $0 \times 1 = \boxed{}$ 3) $0 \times 2 = \boxed{}$

4) $8 \times 0 = \boxed{}$ 5) $5 \times 1 = \boxed{}$ 6) $1 \times 3 = \boxed{}$

7) $1 \times 0 = \boxed{}$ 8) $3 \times 1 = \boxed{}$ 9) $1 \times 1 = \boxed{}$

10) $0 \times 9 = \boxed{}$ 11) $2 \times 0 = \boxed{}$ 12) $1 \times 3 = \boxed{}$

13) $1 \times 7 = \boxed{}$ 14) $6 \times 0 = \boxed{}$ 15) $1 \times 2 = \boxed{}$

16)
$$\begin{array}{r} 1 \\ \times\ 2 \\ \hline \end{array}$$

17)
$$\begin{array}{r} 4 \\ \times\ 1 \\ \hline \end{array}$$

18)
$$\begin{array}{r} 1 \\ \times\ 5 \\ \hline \end{array}$$

19)
$$\begin{array}{r} 0 \\ \times\ 3 \\ \hline \end{array}$$

20)
$$\begin{array}{r} 1 \\ \times\ 4 \\ \hline \end{array}$$

21)
$$\begin{array}{r} 0 \\ \times\ 3 \\ \hline \end{array}$$

22)
$$\begin{array}{r} 0 \\ \times\ 4 \\ \hline \end{array}$$

23)
$$\begin{array}{r} 7 \\ \times\ 1 \\ \hline \end{array}$$

24)
$$\begin{array}{r} 0 \\ \times\ 9 \\ \hline \end{array}$$

25)
$$\begin{array}{r} 3 \\ \times\ 0 \\ \hline \end{array}$$

26)
$$\begin{array}{r} 7 \\ \times\ 1 \\ \hline \end{array}$$

27)
$$\begin{array}{r} 1 \\ \times\ 5 \\ \hline \end{array}$$

28)
$$\begin{array}{r} 0 \\ \times\ 3 \\ \hline \end{array}$$

29)
$$\begin{array}{r} 0 \\ \times\ 4 \\ \hline \end{array}$$

30)
$$\begin{array}{r} 1 \\ \times\ 2 \\ \hline \end{array}$$

31)
$$\begin{array}{r} 3 \\ \times\ 0 \\ \hline \end{array}$$

32)
$$\begin{array}{r} 0 \\ \times\ 2 \\ \hline \end{array}$$

33)
$$\begin{array}{r} 0 \\ \times\ 4 \\ \hline \end{array}$$

34)
$$\begin{array}{r} 2 \\ \times\ 0 \\ \hline \end{array}$$

35)
$$\begin{array}{r} 0 \\ \times\ 0 \\ \hline \end{array}$$

Let's Multiply 0 & 1

1) $1 \times 6 =$ ☐   2) $1 \times 7 =$ ☐   3) $9 \times 0 =$ ☐

4) $3 \times 1 =$ ☐   5) $1 \times 0 =$ ☐   6) $1 \times 8 =$ ☐

7) $5 \times 0 =$ ☐   8) $1 \times 1 =$ ☐   9) $1 \times 6 =$ ☐

10) $1 \times 4 =$ ☐   11) $5 \times 0 =$ ☐   12) $2 \times 0 =$ ☐

13) $0 \times 4 =$ ☐   14) $0 \times 0 =$ ☐   15) $1 \times 6 =$ ☐

16)
$$\begin{array}{r} 1 \\ \times\ 1 \\ \hline \square \end{array}$$
17)
$$\begin{array}{r} 5 \\ \times\ 1 \\ \hline \square \end{array}$$
18)
$$\begin{array}{r} 0 \\ \times\ 0 \\ \hline \square \end{array}$$
19)
$$\begin{array}{r} 1 \\ \times\ 6 \\ \hline \square \end{array}$$
20)
$$\begin{array}{r} 1 \\ \times\ 1 \\ \hline \square \end{array}$$

21)
$$\begin{array}{r} 1 \\ \times\ 8 \\ \hline \square \end{array}$$
22)
$$\begin{array}{r} 4 \\ \times\ 0 \\ \hline \square \end{array}$$
23)
$$\begin{array}{r} 1 \\ \times\ 8 \\ \hline \square \end{array}$$
24)
$$\begin{array}{r} 7 \\ \times\ 0 \\ \hline \square \end{array}$$
25)
$$\begin{array}{r} 1 \\ \times\ 1 \\ \hline \square \end{array}$$

26)
$$\begin{array}{r} 5 \\ \times\ 0 \\ \hline \square \end{array}$$
27)
$$\begin{array}{r} 6 \\ \times\ 1 \\ \hline \square \end{array}$$
28)
$$\begin{array}{r} 7 \\ \times\ 0 \\ \hline \square \end{array}$$
29)
$$\begin{array}{r} 3 \\ \times\ 1 \\ \hline \square \end{array}$$
30)
$$\begin{array}{r} 0 \\ \times\ 9 \\ \hline \square \end{array}$$

31)
$$\begin{array}{r} 5 \\ \times\ 0 \\ \hline \square \end{array}$$
32)
$$\begin{array}{r} 0 \\ \times\ 4 \\ \hline \square \end{array}$$
33)
$$\begin{array}{r} 1 \\ \times\ 4 \\ \hline \square \end{array}$$
34)
$$\begin{array}{r} 4 \\ \times\ 0 \\ \hline \square \end{array}$$
35)
$$\begin{array}{r} 3 \\ \times\ 0 \\ \hline \square \end{array}$$

Let's Multiply 0 & 1

1) $6 \times 1 = \boxed{}$ 2) $3 \times 1 = \boxed{}$ 3) $3 \times 0 = \boxed{}$

4) $0 \times 0 = \boxed{}$ 5) $4 \times 1 = \boxed{}$ 6) $0 \times 0 = \boxed{}$

7) $7 \times 1 = \boxed{}$ 8) $0 \times 0 = \boxed{}$ 9) $6 \times 0 = \boxed{}$

10) $2 \times 1 = \boxed{}$ 11) $3 \times 0 = \boxed{}$ 12) $0 \times 1 = \boxed{}$

13) $9 \times 1 = \boxed{}$ 14) $1 \times 1 = \boxed{}$ 15) $4 \times 1 = \boxed{}$

16) 0×6 17) 5×0 18) 0×3 19) 8×0 20) 6×0

21) 0×3 22) 1×0 23) 1×3 24) 1×9 25) 1×0

26) 1×4 27) 0×0 28) 0×5 29) 1×7 30) 4×1

31) 4×0 32) 0×0 33) 1×6 34) 9×0 35) 1×9

Let's Multiply 0 & 1

1) $0 \times 0 = \boxed{}$ 2) $0 \times 0 = \boxed{}$ 3) $1 \times 7 = \boxed{}$

4) $0 \times 6 = \boxed{}$ 5) $0 \times 3 = \boxed{}$ 6) $3 \times 1 = \boxed{}$

7) $1 \times 1 = \boxed{}$ 8) $0 \times 8 = \boxed{}$ 9) $9 \times 0 = \boxed{}$

10) $3 \times 0 = \boxed{}$ 11) $1 \times 0 = \boxed{}$ 12) $1 \times 5 = \boxed{}$

13) $1 \times 5 = \boxed{}$ 14) $9 \times 0 = \boxed{}$ 15) $1 \times 0 = \boxed{}$

16) $\begin{array}{r} 1 \\ \times\, 2 \\ \hline \boxed{} \end{array}$ 17) $\begin{array}{r} 8 \\ \times\, 1 \\ \hline \boxed{} \end{array}$ 18) $\begin{array}{r} 6 \\ \times\, 0 \\ \hline \boxed{} \end{array}$ 19) $\begin{array}{r} 3 \\ \times\, 0 \\ \hline \boxed{} \end{array}$ 20) $\begin{array}{r} 8 \\ \times\, 1 \\ \hline \boxed{} \end{array}$

21) $\begin{array}{r} 0 \\ \times\, 1 \\ \hline \boxed{} \end{array}$ 22) $\begin{array}{r} 1 \\ \times\, 6 \\ \hline \boxed{} \end{array}$ 23) $\begin{array}{r} 0 \\ \times\, 2 \\ \hline \boxed{} \end{array}$ 24) $\begin{array}{r} 0 \\ \times\, 8 \\ \hline \boxed{} \end{array}$ 25) $\begin{array}{r} 1 \\ \times\, 8 \\ \hline \boxed{} \end{array}$

26) $\begin{array}{r} 2 \\ \times\, 0 \\ \hline \boxed{} \end{array}$ 27) $\begin{array}{r} 8 \\ \times\, 0 \\ \hline \boxed{} \end{array}$ 28) $\begin{array}{r} 0 \\ \times\, 8 \\ \hline \boxed{} \end{array}$ 29) $\begin{array}{r} 1 \\ \times\, 6 \\ \hline \boxed{} \end{array}$ 30) $\begin{array}{r} 4 \\ \times\, 1 \\ \hline \boxed{} \end{array}$

31) $\begin{array}{r} 0 \\ \times\, 0 \\ \hline \boxed{} \end{array}$ 32) $\begin{array}{r} 2 \\ \times\, 0 \\ \hline \boxed{} \end{array}$ 33) $\begin{array}{r} 0 \\ \times\, 0 \\ \hline \boxed{} \end{array}$ 34) $\begin{array}{r} 1 \\ \times\, 2 \\ \hline \boxed{} \end{array}$ 35) $\begin{array}{r} 9 \\ \times\, 0 \\ \hline \boxed{} \end{array}$

Let's Multiply 2

1) $2 \times 6 =$ ☐ 2) $2 \times 9 =$ ☐ 3) $2 \times 5 =$ ☐

4) $3 \times 2 =$ ☐ 5) $1 \times 2 =$ ☐ 6) $2 \times 7 =$ ☐

7) $2 \times 1 =$ ☐ 8) $9 \times 2 =$ ☐ 9) $2 \times 7 =$ ☐

10) $2 \times 6 =$ ☐ 11) $3 \times 2 =$ ☐ 12) $6 \times 2 =$ ☐

13) $1 \times 2 =$ ☐ 14) $2 \times 7 =$ ☐ 15) $2 \times 0 =$ ☐

16) $\begin{array}{r} 2 \\ \times\ 3 \\ \hline \end{array}$ 17) $\begin{array}{r} 8 \\ \times\ 2 \\ \hline \end{array}$ 18) $\begin{array}{r} 2 \\ \times\ 2 \\ \hline \end{array}$ 19) $\begin{array}{r} 2 \\ \times\ 2 \\ \hline \end{array}$ 20) $\begin{array}{r} 1 \\ \times\ 2 \\ \hline \end{array}$

21) $\begin{array}{r} 2 \\ \times\ 1 \\ \hline \end{array}$ 22) $\begin{array}{r} 7 \\ \times\ 2 \\ \hline \end{array}$ 23) $\begin{array}{r} 5 \\ \times\ 2 \\ \hline \end{array}$ 24) $\begin{array}{r} 3 \\ \times\ 2 \\ \hline \end{array}$ 25) $\begin{array}{r} 1 \\ \times\ 2 \\ \hline \end{array}$

26) $\begin{array}{r} 1 \\ \times\ 2 \\ \hline \end{array}$ 27) $\begin{array}{r} 4 \\ \times\ 2 \\ \hline \end{array}$ 28) $\begin{array}{r} 4 \\ \times\ 2 \\ \hline \end{array}$ 29) $\begin{array}{r} 2 \\ \times\ 6 \\ \hline \end{array}$ 30) $\begin{array}{r} 2 \\ \times\ 2 \\ \hline \end{array}$

31) $\begin{array}{r} 1 \\ \times\ 2 \\ \hline \end{array}$ 32) $\begin{array}{r} 2 \\ \times\ 5 \\ \hline \end{array}$ 33) $\begin{array}{r} 2 \\ \times\ 2 \\ \hline \end{array}$ 34) $\begin{array}{r} 8 \\ \times\ 2 \\ \hline \end{array}$ 35) $\begin{array}{r} 2 \\ \times\ 5 \\ \hline \end{array}$

Let's Multiply 2

1) $1 \times 2 = \boxed{}$ 2) $3 \times 2 = \boxed{}$ 3) $2 \times 9 = \boxed{}$

4) $2 \times 5 = \boxed{}$ 5) $5 \times 2 = \boxed{}$ 6) $2 \times 9 = \boxed{}$

7) $4 \times 2 = \boxed{}$ 8) $2 \times 0 = \boxed{}$ 9) $3 \times 2 = \boxed{}$

10) $2 \times 6 = \boxed{}$ 11) $2 \times 4 = \boxed{}$ 12) $9 \times 2 = \boxed{}$

13) $8 \times 2 = \boxed{}$ 14) $7 \times 2 = \boxed{}$ 15) $4 \times 2 = \boxed{}$

16)
$$\begin{array}{r} 9 \\ \times\ 2 \\ \hline \end{array}$$

17)
$$\begin{array}{r} 7 \\ \times\ 2 \\ \hline \end{array}$$

18)
$$\begin{array}{r} 8 \\ \times\ 2 \\ \hline \end{array}$$

19)
$$\begin{array}{r} 2 \\ \times\ 7 \\ \hline \end{array}$$

20)
$$\begin{array}{r} 2 \\ \times\ 1 \\ \hline \end{array}$$

21)
$$\begin{array}{r} 2 \\ \times\ 7 \\ \hline \end{array}$$

22)
$$\begin{array}{r} 7 \\ \times\ 2 \\ \hline \end{array}$$

23)
$$\begin{array}{r} 7 \\ \times\ 2 \\ \hline \end{array}$$

24)
$$\begin{array}{r} 2 \\ \times\ 9 \\ \hline \end{array}$$

25)
$$\begin{array}{r} 2 \\ \times\ 0 \\ \hline \end{array}$$

26)
$$\begin{array}{r} 2 \\ \times\ 6 \\ \hline \end{array}$$

27)
$$\begin{array}{r} 7 \\ \times\ 2 \\ \hline \end{array}$$

28)
$$\begin{array}{r} 2 \\ \times\ 3 \\ \hline \end{array}$$

29)
$$\begin{array}{r} 2 \\ \times\ 8 \\ \hline \end{array}$$

30)
$$\begin{array}{r} 2 \\ \times\ 7 \\ \hline \end{array}$$

31)
$$\begin{array}{r} 2 \\ \times\ 5 \\ \hline \end{array}$$

32)
$$\begin{array}{r} 3 \\ \times\ 2 \\ \hline \end{array}$$

33)
$$\begin{array}{r} 2 \\ \times\ 3 \\ \hline \end{array}$$

34)
$$\begin{array}{r} 6 \\ \times\ 2 \\ \hline \end{array}$$

35)
$$\begin{array}{r} 2 \\ \times\ 4 \\ \hline \end{array}$$

Let's Multiply 2

1) $2 \times 1 = \boxed{}$ 2) $2 \times 8 = \boxed{}$ 3) $2 \times 8 = \boxed{}$

4) $7 \times 2 = \boxed{}$ 5) $1 \times 2 = \boxed{}$ 6) $0 \times 2 = \boxed{}$

7) $2 \times 3 = \boxed{}$ 8) $7 \times 2 = \boxed{}$ 9) $2 \times 6 = \boxed{}$

10) $3 \times 2 = \boxed{}$ 11) $2 \times 3 = \boxed{}$ 12) $6 \times 2 = \boxed{}$

13) $8 \times 2 = \boxed{}$ 14) $7 \times 2 = \boxed{}$ 15) $4 \times 2 = \boxed{}$

16) $\begin{array}{r} 8 \\ \times\ 2 \\ \hline \end{array}$ 17) $\begin{array}{r} 2 \\ \times\ 9 \\ \hline \end{array}$ 18) $\begin{array}{r} 2 \\ \times\ 4 \\ \hline \end{array}$ 19) $\begin{array}{r} 2 \\ \times\ 0 \\ \hline \end{array}$ 20) $\begin{array}{r} 4 \\ \times\ 2 \\ \hline \end{array}$

21) $\begin{array}{r} 2 \\ \times\ 6 \\ \hline \end{array}$ 22) $\begin{array}{r} 2 \\ \times\ 2 \\ \hline \end{array}$ 23) $\begin{array}{r} 2 \\ \times\ 2 \\ \hline \end{array}$ 24) $\begin{array}{r} 3 \\ \times\ 2 \\ \hline \end{array}$ 25) $\begin{array}{r} 2 \\ \times\ 8 \\ \hline \end{array}$

26) $\begin{array}{r} 4 \\ \times\ 2 \\ \hline \end{array}$ 27) $\begin{array}{r} 3 \\ \times\ 2 \\ \hline \end{array}$ 28) $\begin{array}{r} 7 \\ \times\ 2 \\ \hline \end{array}$ 29) $\begin{array}{r} 2 \\ \times\ 8 \\ \hline \end{array}$ 30) $\begin{array}{r} 2 \\ \times\ 8 \\ \hline \end{array}$

31) $\begin{array}{r} 1 \\ \times\ 2 \\ \hline \end{array}$ 32) $\begin{array}{r} 2 \\ \times\ 5 \\ \hline \end{array}$ 33) $\begin{array}{r} 6 \\ \times\ 2 \\ \hline \end{array}$ 34) $\begin{array}{r} 0 \\ \times\ 2 \\ \hline \end{array}$ 35) $\begin{array}{r} 9 \\ \times\ 2 \\ \hline \end{array}$

Let's Multiply 2

1) $3 \times 2 = \boxed{}$ 2) $5 \times 2 = \boxed{}$ 3) $2 \times 4 = \boxed{}$

4) $2 \times 4 = \boxed{}$ 5) $1 \times 2 = \boxed{}$ 6) $2 \times 5 = \boxed{}$

7) $2 \times 4 = \boxed{}$ 8) $9 \times 2 = \boxed{}$ 9) $2 \times 8 = \boxed{}$

10) $5 \times 2 = \boxed{}$ 11) $2 \times 9 = \boxed{}$ 12) $2 \times 8 = \boxed{}$

13) $2 \times 2 = \boxed{}$ 14) $3 \times 2 = \boxed{}$ 15) $2 \times 4 = \boxed{}$

16) $\begin{array}{r} 2 \\ \times\ 2 \\ \hline \end{array}$ 17) $\begin{array}{r} 2 \\ \times\ 3 \\ \hline \end{array}$ 18) $\begin{array}{r} 2 \\ \times\ 7 \\ \hline \end{array}$ 19) $\begin{array}{r} 2 \\ \times\ 0 \\ \hline \end{array}$ 20) $\begin{array}{r} 2 \\ \times\ 2 \\ \hline \end{array}$

21) $\begin{array}{r} 2 \\ \times\ 6 \\ \hline \end{array}$ 22) $\begin{array}{r} 2 \\ \times\ 2 \\ \hline \end{array}$ 23) $\begin{array}{r} 2 \\ \times\ 2 \\ \hline \end{array}$ 24) $\begin{array}{r} 2 \\ \times\ 7 \\ \hline \end{array}$ 25) $\begin{array}{r} 2 \\ \times\ 8 \\ \hline \end{array}$

26) $\begin{array}{r} 2 \\ \times\ 8 \\ \hline \end{array}$ 27) $\begin{array}{r} 2 \\ \times\ 9 \\ \hline \end{array}$ 28) $\begin{array}{r} 3 \\ \times\ 2 \\ \hline \end{array}$ 29) $\begin{array}{r} 2 \\ \times\ 2 \\ \hline \end{array}$ 30) $\begin{array}{r} 2 \\ \times\ 8 \\ \hline \end{array}$

31) $\begin{array}{r} 2 \\ \times\ 7 \\ \hline \end{array}$ 32) $\begin{array}{r} 9 \\ \times\ 2 \\ \hline \end{array}$ 33) $\begin{array}{r} 2 \\ \times\ 6 \\ \hline \end{array}$ 34) $\begin{array}{r} 2 \\ \times\ 4 \\ \hline \end{array}$ 35) $\begin{array}{r} 2 \\ \times\ 1 \\ \hline \end{array}$

Let's Multiply 3

1) $3 \times 9 = \boxed{}$ 2) $2 \times 3 = \boxed{}$ 3) $2 \times 3 = \boxed{}$

4) $3 \times 9 = \boxed{}$ 5) $5 \times 3 = \boxed{}$ 6) $3 \times 6 = \boxed{}$

7) $8 \times 3 = \boxed{}$ 8) $3 \times 7 = \boxed{}$ 9) $3 \times 9 = \boxed{}$

10) $3 \times 3 = \boxed{}$ 11) $3 \times 3 = \boxed{}$ 12) $1 \times 3 = \boxed{}$

13) $4 \times 3 = \boxed{}$ 14) $3 \times 9 = \boxed{}$ 15) $4 \times 3 = \boxed{}$

16)
$$\begin{array}{r} 0 \\ \times\ 3 \\ \hline \end{array}$$

17)
$$\begin{array}{r} 3 \\ \times\ 6 \\ \hline \end{array}$$

18)
$$\begin{array}{r} 3 \\ \times\ 7 \\ \hline \end{array}$$

19)
$$\begin{array}{r} 8 \\ \times\ 3 \\ \hline \end{array}$$

20)
$$\begin{array}{r} 3 \\ \times\ 5 \\ \hline \end{array}$$

21)
$$\begin{array}{r} 5 \\ \times\ 3 \\ \hline \end{array}$$

22)
$$\begin{array}{r} 3 \\ \times\ 2 \\ \hline \end{array}$$

23)
$$\begin{array}{r} 5 \\ \times\ 3 \\ \hline \end{array}$$

24)
$$\begin{array}{r} 6 \\ \times\ 3 \\ \hline \end{array}$$

25)
$$\begin{array}{r} 3 \\ \times\ 8 \\ \hline \end{array}$$

26)
$$\begin{array}{r} 5 \\ \times\ 3 \\ \hline \end{array}$$

27)
$$\begin{array}{r} 7 \\ \times\ 3 \\ \hline \end{array}$$

28)
$$\begin{array}{r} 1 \\ \times\ 3 \\ \hline \end{array}$$

29)
$$\begin{array}{r} 3 \\ \times\ 7 \\ \hline \end{array}$$

30)
$$\begin{array}{r} 3 \\ \times\ 4 \\ \hline \end{array}$$

31)
$$\begin{array}{r} 3 \\ \times\ 6 \\ \hline \end{array}$$

32)
$$\begin{array}{r} 5 \\ \times\ 3 \\ \hline \end{array}$$

33)
$$\begin{array}{r} 3 \\ \times\ 2 \\ \hline \end{array}$$

34)
$$\begin{array}{r} 3 \\ \times\ 3 \\ \hline \end{array}$$

35)
$$\begin{array}{r} 3 \\ \times\ 3 \\ \hline \end{array}$$

Let's Multiply 3

1) $3 \times 6 =$ ☐   2) $9 \times 3 =$ ☐   3) $3 \times 7 =$ ☐

4) $3 \times 3 =$ ☐   5) $3 \times 7 =$ ☐   6) $8 \times 3 =$ ☐

7) $1 \times 3 =$ ☐   8) $3 \times 6 =$ ☐   9) $3 \times 9 =$ ☐

10) $9 \times 3 =$ ☐   11) $7 \times 3 =$ ☐   12) $3 \times 9 =$ ☐

13) $9 \times 3 =$ ☐   14) $3 \times 6 =$ ☐   15) $6 \times 3 =$ ☐

16) $\begin{array}{r} 3 \\ \times\ 0 \\ \hline \end{array}$ 17) $\begin{array}{r} 9 \\ \times\ 3 \\ \hline \end{array}$ 18) $\begin{array}{r} 3 \\ \times\ 6 \\ \hline \end{array}$ 19) $\begin{array}{r} 4 \\ \times\ 3 \\ \hline \end{array}$ 20) $\begin{array}{r} 1 \\ \times\ 3 \\ \hline \end{array}$

21) $\begin{array}{r} 3 \\ \times\ 3 \\ \hline \end{array}$ 22) $\begin{array}{r} 2 \\ \times\ 3 \\ \hline \end{array}$ 23) $\begin{array}{r} 3 \\ \times\ 5 \\ \hline \end{array}$ 24) $\begin{array}{r} 3 \\ \times\ 1 \\ \hline \end{array}$ 25) $\begin{array}{r} 3 \\ \times\ 4 \\ \hline \end{array}$

26) $\begin{array}{r} 3 \\ \times\ 8 \\ \hline \end{array}$ 27) $\begin{array}{r} 3 \\ \times\ 3 \\ \hline \end{array}$ 28) $\begin{array}{r} 3 \\ \times\ 9 \\ \hline \end{array}$ 29) $\begin{array}{r} 2 \\ \times\ 3 \\ \hline \end{array}$ 30) $\begin{array}{r} 3 \\ \times\ 3 \\ \hline \end{array}$

31) $\begin{array}{r} 3 \\ \times\ 6 \\ \hline \end{array}$ 32) $\begin{array}{r} 3 \\ \times\ 3 \\ \hline \end{array}$ 33) $\begin{array}{r} 3 \\ \times\ 2 \\ \hline \end{array}$ 34) $\begin{array}{r} 6 \\ \times\ 3 \\ \hline \end{array}$ 35) $\begin{array}{r} 3 \\ \times\ 5 \\ \hline \end{array}$

Let's Multiply 3

1) $3 \times 3 =$ ☐   2) $9 \times 3 =$ ☐   3) $3 \times 3 =$ ☐

4) $1 \times 3 =$ ☐   5) $3 \times 8 =$ ☐   6) $3 \times 2 =$ ☐

7) $3 \times 8 =$ ☐   8) $3 \times 2 =$ ☐   9) $3 \times 6 =$ ☐

10) $3 \times 4 =$ ☐   11) $3 \times 6 =$ ☐   12) $5 \times 3 =$ ☐

13) $3 \times 4 =$ ☐   14) $3 \times 3 =$ ☐   15) $3 \times 0 =$ ☐

16) $\begin{array}{r} 3 \\ \times\ 5 \\ \hline \end{array}$ 17) $\begin{array}{r} 3 \\ \times\ 9 \\ \hline \end{array}$ 18) $\begin{array}{r} 3 \\ \times\ 9 \\ \hline \end{array}$ 19) $\begin{array}{r} 3 \\ \times\ 3 \\ \hline \end{array}$ 20) $\begin{array}{r} 2 \\ \times\ 3 \\ \hline \end{array}$

21) $\begin{array}{r} 3 \\ \times\ 8 \\ \hline \end{array}$ 22) $\begin{array}{r} 3 \\ \times\ 3 \\ \hline \end{array}$ 23) $\begin{array}{r} 3 \\ \times\ 4 \\ \hline \end{array}$ 24) $\begin{array}{r} 3 \\ \times\ 9 \\ \hline \end{array}$ 25) $\begin{array}{r} 6 \\ \times\ 3 \\ \hline \end{array}$

26) $\begin{array}{r} 3 \\ \times\ 7 \\ \hline \end{array}$ 27) $\begin{array}{r} 9 \\ \times\ 3 \\ \hline \end{array}$ 28) $\begin{array}{r} 4 \\ \times\ 3 \\ \hline \end{array}$ 29) $\begin{array}{r} 3 \\ \times\ 0 \\ \hline \end{array}$ 30) $\begin{array}{r} 3 \\ \times\ 6 \\ \hline \end{array}$

31) $\begin{array}{r} 4 \\ \times\ 3 \\ \hline \end{array}$ 32) $\begin{array}{r} 6 \\ \times\ 3 \\ \hline \end{array}$ 33) $\begin{array}{r} 3 \\ \times\ 3 \\ \hline \end{array}$ 34) $\begin{array}{r} 9 \\ \times\ 3 \\ \hline \end{array}$ 35) $\begin{array}{r} 3 \\ \times\ 7 \\ \hline \end{array}$

Let's Multiply 3

1) 3 × 9 = ☐ 2) 3 × 4 = ☐ 3) 3 × 2 = ☐

4) 3 × 7 = ☐ 5) 9 × 3 = ☐ 6) 6 × 3 = ☐

7) 3 × 9 = ☐ 8) 5 × 3 = ☐ 9) 3 × 0 = ☐

10) 0 × 3 = ☐ 11) 3 × 8 = ☐ 12) 3 × 0 = ☐

13) 3 × 9 = ☐ 14) 3 × 7 = ☐ 15) 2 × 3 = ☐

16) 3 × 1 17) 3 × 7 18) 3 × 7 19) 7 × 3 20) 3 × 6

21) 1 × 3 22) 3 × 0 23) 3 × 4 24) 3 × 5 25) 3 × 4

26) 3 × 8 27) 3 × 9 28) 8 × 3 29) 3 × 8 30) 3 × 3

31) 3 × 9 32) 7 × 3 33) 3 × 6 34) 3 × 0 35) 3 × 0

Let's Multiply 4

1) $4 \times 3 = \boxed{}$ 2) $6 \times 4 = \boxed{}$ 3) $4 \times 9 = \boxed{}$

4) $0 \times 4 = \boxed{}$ 5) $4 \times 4 = \boxed{}$ 6) $5 \times 4 = \boxed{}$

7) $7 \times 4 = \boxed{}$ 8) $5 \times 4 = \boxed{}$ 9) $4 \times 1 = \boxed{}$

10) $0 \times 4 = \boxed{}$ 11) $9 \times 4 = \boxed{}$ 12) $4 \times 5 = \boxed{}$

13) $5 \times 4 = \boxed{}$ 14) $4 \times 4 = \boxed{}$ 15) $5 \times 4 = \boxed{}$

16) $\begin{array}{r} 4 \\ \times\ 0 \\ \hline \end{array}$ 17) $\begin{array}{r} 4 \\ \times\ 8 \\ \hline \end{array}$ 18) $\begin{array}{r} 8 \\ \times\ 4 \\ \hline \end{array}$ 19) $\begin{array}{r} 4 \\ \times\ 6 \\ \hline \end{array}$ 20) $\begin{array}{r} 4 \\ \times\ 7 \\ \hline \end{array}$

21) $\begin{array}{r} 5 \\ \times\ 4 \\ \hline \end{array}$ 22) $\begin{array}{r} 4 \\ \times\ 0 \\ \hline \end{array}$ 23) $\begin{array}{r} 4 \\ \times\ 2 \\ \hline \end{array}$ 24) $\begin{array}{r} 4 \\ \times\ 9 \\ \hline \end{array}$ 25) $\begin{array}{r} 3 \\ \times\ 4 \\ \hline \end{array}$

26) $\begin{array}{r} 3 \\ \times\ 4 \\ \hline \end{array}$ 27) $\begin{array}{r} 4 \\ \times\ 4 \\ \hline \end{array}$ 28) $\begin{array}{r} 4 \\ \times\ 5 \\ \hline \end{array}$ 29) $\begin{array}{r} 4 \\ \times\ 8 \\ \hline \end{array}$ 30) $\begin{array}{r} 4 \\ \times\ 9 \\ \hline \end{array}$

31) $\begin{array}{r} 0 \\ \times\ 4 \\ \hline \end{array}$ 32) $\begin{array}{r} 7 \\ \times\ 4 \\ \hline \end{array}$ 33) $\begin{array}{r} 4 \\ \times\ 9 \\ \hline \end{array}$ 34) $\begin{array}{r} 4 \\ \times\ 5 \\ \hline \end{array}$ 35) $\begin{array}{r} 4 \\ \times\ 5 \\ \hline \end{array}$

Let's Multiply 4

1) $4 \times 4 =$ ☐ 2) $6 \times 4 =$ ☐ 3) $6 \times 4 =$ ☐

4) $4 \times 6 =$ ☐ 5) $4 \times 4 =$ ☐ 6) $4 \times 6 =$ ☐

7) $4 \times 3 =$ ☐ 8) $5 \times 4 =$ ☐ 9) $4 \times 2 =$ ☐

10) $4 \times 8 =$ ☐ 11) $0 \times 4 =$ ☐ 12) $4 \times 6 =$ ☐

13) $5 \times 4 =$ ☐ 14) $7 \times 4 =$ ☐ 15) $5 \times 4 =$ ☐

16)
$$\begin{array}{r} 6 \\ \times\ 4 \\ \hline \end{array}$$
17)
$$\begin{array}{r} 4 \\ \times\ 7 \\ \hline \end{array}$$
18)
$$\begin{array}{r} 4 \\ \times\ 2 \\ \hline \end{array}$$
19)
$$\begin{array}{r} 4 \\ \times\ 2 \\ \hline \end{array}$$
20)
$$\begin{array}{r} 7 \\ \times\ 4 \\ \hline \end{array}$$

21)
$$\begin{array}{r} 9 \\ \times\ 4 \\ \hline \end{array}$$
22)
$$\begin{array}{r} 4 \\ \times\ 4 \\ \hline \end{array}$$
23)
$$\begin{array}{r} 3 \\ \times\ 4 \\ \hline \end{array}$$
24)
$$\begin{array}{r} 3 \\ \times\ 4 \\ \hline \end{array}$$
25)
$$\begin{array}{r} 4 \\ \times\ 9 \\ \hline \end{array}$$

26)
$$\begin{array}{r} 0 \\ \times\ 4 \\ \hline \end{array}$$
27)
$$\begin{array}{r} 1 \\ \times\ 4 \\ \hline \end{array}$$
28)
$$\begin{array}{r} 4 \\ \times\ 4 \\ \hline \end{array}$$
29)
$$\begin{array}{r} 5 \\ \times\ 4 \\ \hline \end{array}$$
30)
$$\begin{array}{r} 4 \\ \times\ 0 \\ \hline \end{array}$$

31)
$$\begin{array}{r} 6 \\ \times\ 4 \\ \hline \end{array}$$
32)
$$\begin{array}{r} 1 \\ \times\ 4 \\ \hline \end{array}$$
33)
$$\begin{array}{r} 4 \\ \times\ 4 \\ \hline \end{array}$$
34)
$$\begin{array}{r} 4 \\ \times\ 6 \\ \hline \end{array}$$
35)
$$\begin{array}{r} 4 \\ \times\ 8 \\ \hline \end{array}$$

Let's Multiply 4

1) $4 \times 4 =$ ☐   2) $0 \times 4 =$ ☐   3) $4 \times 1 =$ ☐

4) $9 \times 4 =$ ☐   5) $4 \times 1 =$ ☐   6) $8 \times 4 =$ ☐

7) $7 \times 4 =$ ☐   8) $8 \times 4 =$ ☐   9) $4 \times 3 =$ ☐

10) $7 \times 4 =$ ☐   11) $3 \times 4 =$ ☐   12) $4 \times 6 =$ ☐

13) $4 \times 7 =$ ☐   14) $4 \times 6 =$ ☐   15) $4 \times 8 =$ ☐

16) $\begin{array}{r} 4 \\ \times\ 1 \\ \hline \end{array}$ 17) $\begin{array}{r} 0 \\ \times\ 4 \\ \hline \end{array}$ 18) $\begin{array}{r} 8 \\ \times\ 4 \\ \hline \end{array}$ 19) $\begin{array}{r} 4 \\ \times\ 2 \\ \hline \end{array}$ 20) $\begin{array}{r} 4 \\ \times\ 4 \\ \hline \end{array}$

21) $\begin{array}{r} 0 \\ \times\ 4 \\ \hline \end{array}$ 22) $\begin{array}{r} 4 \\ \times\ 0 \\ \hline \end{array}$ 23) $\begin{array}{r} 5 \\ \times\ 4 \\ \hline \end{array}$ 24) $\begin{array}{r} 7 \\ \times\ 4 \\ \hline \end{array}$ 25) $\begin{array}{r} 3 \\ \times\ 4 \\ \hline \end{array}$

26) $\begin{array}{r} 4 \\ \times\ 9 \\ \hline \end{array}$ 27) $\begin{array}{r} 5 \\ \times\ 4 \\ \hline \end{array}$ 28) $\begin{array}{r} 4 \\ \times\ 3 \\ \hline \end{array}$ 29) $\begin{array}{r} 1 \\ \times\ 4 \\ \hline \end{array}$ 30) $\begin{array}{r} 4 \\ \times\ 0 \\ \hline \end{array}$

31) $\begin{array}{r} 8 \\ \times\ 4 \\ \hline \end{array}$ 32) $\begin{array}{r} 4 \\ \times\ 4 \\ \hline \end{array}$ 33) $\begin{array}{r} 4 \\ \times\ 3 \\ \hline \end{array}$ 34) $\begin{array}{r} 4 \\ \times\ 5 \\ \hline \end{array}$ 35) $\begin{array}{r} 4 \\ \times\ 1 \\ \hline \end{array}$

Let's Multiply 4

1) $3 \times 4 = $ [ ]   2) $4 \times 7 = $ [ ]   3) $4 \times 3 = $ [ ]

4) $2 \times 4 = $ [ ]   5) $4 \times 5 = $ [ ]   6) $4 \times 1 = $ [ ]

7) $5 \times 4 = $ [ ]   8) $8 \times 4 = $ [ ]   9) $4 \times 5 = $ [ ]

10) $4 \times 4 = $ [ ]   11) $4 \times 3 = $ [ ]   12) $4 \times 9 = $ [ ]

13) $4 \times 6 = $ [ ]   14) $3 \times 4 = $ [ ]   15) $4 \times 8 = $ [ ]

16)
$$\begin{array}{r} 4 \\ \times\ 2 \\ \hline \end{array}$$

17)
$$\begin{array}{r} 5 \\ \times\ 4 \\ \hline \end{array}$$

18)
$$\begin{array}{r} 4 \\ \times\ 6 \\ \hline \end{array}$$

19)
$$\begin{array}{r} 0 \\ \times\ 4 \\ \hline \end{array}$$

20)
$$\begin{array}{r} 4 \\ \times\ 5 \\ \hline \end{array}$$

21)
$$\begin{array}{r} 4 \\ \times\ 2 \\ \hline \end{array}$$

22)
$$\begin{array}{r} 4 \\ \times\ 8 \\ \hline \end{array}$$

23)
$$\begin{array}{r} 4 \\ \times\ 8 \\ \hline \end{array}$$

24)
$$\begin{array}{r} 9 \\ \times\ 4 \\ \hline \end{array}$$

25)
$$\begin{array}{r} 4 \\ \times\ 3 \\ \hline \end{array}$$

26)
$$\begin{array}{r} 9 \\ \times\ 4 \\ \hline \end{array}$$

27)
$$\begin{array}{r} 4 \\ \times\ 4 \\ \hline \end{array}$$

28)
$$\begin{array}{r} 5 \\ \times\ 4 \\ \hline \end{array}$$

29)
$$\begin{array}{r} 5 \\ \times\ 4 \\ \hline \end{array}$$

30)
$$\begin{array}{r} 4 \\ \times\ 4 \\ \hline \end{array}$$

31)
$$\begin{array}{r} 1 \\ \times\ 4 \\ \hline \end{array}$$

32)
$$\begin{array}{r} 7 \\ \times\ 4 \\ \hline \end{array}$$

33)
$$\begin{array}{r} 6 \\ \times\ 4 \\ \hline \end{array}$$

34)
$$\begin{array}{r} 1 \\ \times\ 4 \\ \hline \end{array}$$

35)
$$\begin{array}{r} 3 \\ \times\ 4 \\ \hline \end{array}$$

Let's Multiply 5

1) $5 \times 4 = \boxed{}$ 2) $5 \times 9 = \boxed{}$ 3) $5 \times 9 = \boxed{}$

4) $3 \times 5 = \boxed{}$ 5) $5 \times 7 = \boxed{}$ 6) $5 \times 7 = \boxed{}$

7) $6 \times 5 = \boxed{}$ 8) $5 \times 6 = \boxed{}$ 9) $2 \times 5 = \boxed{}$

10) $5 \times 8 = \boxed{}$ 11) $5 \times 3 = \boxed{}$ 12) $5 \times 8 = \boxed{}$

13) $3 \times 5 = \boxed{}$ 14) $8 \times 5 = \boxed{}$ 15) $9 \times 5 = \boxed{}$

16) 7×5 17) 5×3 18) 3×5 19) 7×5 20) 5×5

21) 0×5 22) 5×8 23) 5×2 24) 5×0 25) 7×5

26) 7×5 27) 5×4 28) 5×2 29) 6×5 30) 1×5

31) 5×8 32) 5×7 33) 9×5 34) 5×5 35) 4×5

Let's Multiply 5

1) $6 \times 5 =$ ☐   2) $1 \times 5 =$ ☐   3) $5 \times 5 =$ ☐

4) $3 \times 5 =$ ☐   5) $5 \times 4 =$ ☐   6) $8 \times 5 =$ ☐

7) $7 \times 5 =$ ☐   8) $2 \times 5 =$ ☐   9) $7 \times 5 =$ ☐

10) $5 \times 2 =$ ☐   11) $2 \times 5 =$ ☐   12) $5 \times 9 =$ ☐

13) $5 \times 1 =$ ☐   14) $5 \times 1 =$ ☐   15) $5 \times 5 =$ ☐

16) $\begin{array}{r} 5 \\ \times\ 5 \\ \hline \end{array}$ 17) $\begin{array}{r} 7 \\ \times\ 5 \\ \hline \end{array}$ 18) $\begin{array}{r} 7 \\ \times\ 5 \\ \hline \end{array}$ 19) $\begin{array}{r} 5 \\ \times\ 4 \\ \hline \end{array}$ 20) $\begin{array}{r} 5 \\ \times\ 2 \\ \hline \end{array}$

21) $\begin{array}{r} 5 \\ \times\ 5 \\ \hline \end{array}$ 22) $\begin{array}{r} 5 \\ \times\ 6 \\ \hline \end{array}$ 23) $\begin{array}{r} 5 \\ \times\ 2 \\ \hline \end{array}$ 24) $\begin{array}{r} 5 \\ \times\ 5 \\ \hline \end{array}$ 25) $\begin{array}{r} 5 \\ \times\ 3 \\ \hline \end{array}$

26) $\begin{array}{r} 5 \\ \times\ 2 \\ \hline \end{array}$ 27) $\begin{array}{r} 3 \\ \times\ 5 \\ \hline \end{array}$ 28) $\begin{array}{r} 5 \\ \times\ 3 \\ \hline \end{array}$ 29) $\begin{array}{r} 5 \\ \times\ 5 \\ \hline \end{array}$ 30) $\begin{array}{r} 2 \\ \times\ 5 \\ \hline \end{array}$

31) $\begin{array}{r} 9 \\ \times\ 5 \\ \hline \end{array}$ 32) $\begin{array}{r} 5 \\ \times\ 0 \\ \hline \end{array}$ 33) $\begin{array}{r} 7 \\ \times\ 5 \\ \hline \end{array}$ 34) $\begin{array}{r} 3 \\ \times\ 5 \\ \hline \end{array}$ 35) $\begin{array}{r} 5 \\ \times\ 5 \\ \hline \end{array}$

Let's Multiply 5

1) $6 \times 5 = \boxed{}$ 2) $5 \times 6 = \boxed{}$ 3) $2 \times 5 = \boxed{}$

4) $5 \times 5 = \boxed{}$ 5) $5 \times 3 = \boxed{}$ 6) $5 \times 3 = \boxed{}$

7) $5 \times 3 = \boxed{}$ 8) $1 \times 5 = \boxed{}$ 9) $6 \times 5 = \boxed{}$

10) $5 \times 7 = \boxed{}$ 11) $2 \times 5 = \boxed{}$ 12) $5 \times 7 = \boxed{}$

13) $5 \times 4 = \boxed{}$ 14) $5 \times 3 = \boxed{}$ 15) $7 \times 5 = \boxed{}$

16) $\begin{array}{r}1\\ \times\ 5\\ \hline\end{array}$ 17) $\begin{array}{r}6\\ \times\ 5\\ \hline\end{array}$ 18) $\begin{array}{r}2\\ \times\ 5\\ \hline\end{array}$ 19) $\begin{array}{r}5\\ \times\ 3\\ \hline\end{array}$ 20) $\begin{array}{r}5\\ \times\ 0\\ \hline\end{array}$

21) $\begin{array}{r}5\\ \times\ 3\\ \hline\end{array}$ 22) $\begin{array}{r}5\\ \times\ 7\\ \hline\end{array}$ 23) $\begin{array}{r}6\\ \times\ 5\\ \hline\end{array}$ 24) $\begin{array}{r}2\\ \times\ 5\\ \hline\end{array}$ 25) $\begin{array}{r}3\\ \times\ 5\\ \hline\end{array}$

26) $\begin{array}{r}5\\ \times\ 2\\ \hline\end{array}$ 27) $\begin{array}{r}5\\ \times\ 5\\ \hline\end{array}$ 28) $\begin{array}{r}5\\ \times\ 9\\ \hline\end{array}$ 29) $\begin{array}{r}5\\ \times\ 6\\ \hline\end{array}$ 30) $\begin{array}{r}2\\ \times\ 5\\ \hline\end{array}$

31) $\begin{array}{r}5\\ \times\ 5\\ \hline\end{array}$ 32) $\begin{array}{r}2\\ \times\ 5\\ \hline\end{array}$ 33) $\begin{array}{r}6\\ \times\ 5\\ \hline\end{array}$ 34) $\begin{array}{r}3\\ \times\ 5\\ \hline\end{array}$ 35) $\begin{array}{r}5\\ \times\ 5\\ \hline\end{array}$

Let's Multiply 5

1) $5 \times 8 =$ ☐   2) $5 \times 2 =$ ☐   3) $5 \times 9 =$ ☐

4) $5 \times 6 =$ ☐   5) $5 \times 6 =$ ☐   6) $3 \times 5 =$ ☐

7) $9 \times 5 =$ ☐   8) $5 \times 5 =$ ☐   9) $5 \times 6 =$ ☐

10) $7 \times 5 =$ ☐   11) $2 \times 5 =$ ☐   12) $4 \times 5 =$ ☐

13) $5 \times 5 =$ ☐   14) $3 \times 5 =$ ☐   15) $5 \times 6 =$ ☐

16) $\begin{array}{r} 2 \\ \times\ 5 \\ \hline \end{array}$ 17) $\begin{array}{r} 8 \\ \times\ 5 \\ \hline \end{array}$ 18) $\begin{array}{r} 5 \\ \times\ 5 \\ \hline \end{array}$ 19) $\begin{array}{r} 5 \\ \times\ 4 \\ \hline \end{array}$ 20) $\begin{array}{r} 5 \\ \times\ 4 \\ \hline \end{array}$

21) $\begin{array}{r} 2 \\ \times\ 5 \\ \hline \end{array}$ 22) $\begin{array}{r} 5 \\ \times\ 0 \\ \hline \end{array}$ 23) $\begin{array}{r} 5 \\ \times\ 2 \\ \hline \end{array}$ 24) $\begin{array}{r} 5 \\ \times\ 6 \\ \hline \end{array}$ 25) $\begin{array}{r} 5 \\ \times\ 9 \\ \hline \end{array}$

26) $\begin{array}{r} 4 \\ \times\ 5 \\ \hline \end{array}$ 27) $\begin{array}{r} 5 \\ \times\ 5 \\ \hline \end{array}$ 28) $\begin{array}{r} 2 \\ \times\ 5 \\ \hline \end{array}$ 29) $\begin{array}{r} 2 \\ \times\ 5 \\ \hline \end{array}$ 30) $\begin{array}{r} 5 \\ \times\ 6 \\ \hline \end{array}$

31) $\begin{array}{r} 5 \\ \times\ 3 \\ \hline \end{array}$ 32) $\begin{array}{r} 5 \\ \times\ 0 \\ \hline \end{array}$ 33) $\begin{array}{r} 2 \\ \times\ 5 \\ \hline \end{array}$ 34) $\begin{array}{r} 5 \\ \times\ 7 \\ \hline \end{array}$ 35) $\begin{array}{r} 5 \\ \times\ 5 \\ \hline \end{array}$

Let's Multiply 6

1) $2 \times 6 = \boxed{}$ 2) $7 \times 6 = \boxed{}$ 3) $4 \times 6 = \boxed{}$

4) $8 \times 6 = \boxed{}$ 5) $6 \times 2 = \boxed{}$ 6) $6 \times 2 = \boxed{}$

7) $2 \times 6 = \boxed{}$ 8) $6 \times 2 = \boxed{}$ 9) $3 \times 6 = \boxed{}$

10) $3 \times 6 = \boxed{}$ 11) $6 \times 4 = \boxed{}$ 12) $6 \times 7 = \boxed{}$

13) $4 \times 6 = \boxed{}$ 14) $7 \times 6 = \boxed{}$ 15) $6 \times 6 = \boxed{}$

16) 6×6 17) 5×6 18) 6×6 19) 6×2 20) 6×8

21) 6×6 22) 6×1 23) 6×7 24) 4×6 25) 1×6

26) 6×2 27) 9×6 28) 6×7 29) 6×2 30) 6×6

31) 6×2 32) 8×6 33) 6×6 34) 8×6 35) 7×6

Let's Multiply 6

1) $4 \times 6 = \boxed{}$ 2) $6 \times 9 = \boxed{}$ 3) $6 \times 5 = \boxed{}$

4) $6 \times 6 = \boxed{}$ 5) $6 \times 0 = \boxed{}$ 6) $6 \times 2 = \boxed{}$

7) $1 \times 6 = \boxed{}$ 8) $6 \times 0 = \boxed{}$ 9) $6 \times 8 = \boxed{}$

10) $4 \times 6 = \boxed{}$ 11) $6 \times 6 = \boxed{}$ 12) $4 \times 6 = \boxed{}$

13) $7 \times 6 = \boxed{}$ 14) $9 \times 6 = \boxed{}$ 15) $6 \times 8 = \boxed{}$

16)
$$\begin{array}{r} 9 \\ \times\ 6 \\ \hline \end{array}$$
17)
$$\begin{array}{r} 6 \\ \times\ 4 \\ \hline \end{array}$$
18)
$$\begin{array}{r} 4 \\ \times\ 6 \\ \hline \end{array}$$
19)
$$\begin{array}{r} 2 \\ \times\ 6 \\ \hline \end{array}$$
20)
$$\begin{array}{r} 5 \\ \times\ 6 \\ \hline \end{array}$$

21)
$$\begin{array}{r} 6 \\ \times\ 4 \\ \hline \end{array}$$
22)
$$\begin{array}{r} 6 \\ \times\ 6 \\ \hline \end{array}$$
23)
$$\begin{array}{r} 6 \\ \times\ 3 \\ \hline \end{array}$$
24)
$$\begin{array}{r} 3 \\ \times\ 6 \\ \hline \end{array}$$
25)
$$\begin{array}{r} 8 \\ \times\ 6 \\ \hline \end{array}$$

26)
$$\begin{array}{r} 6 \\ \times\ 1 \\ \hline \end{array}$$
27)
$$\begin{array}{r} 2 \\ \times\ 6 \\ \hline \end{array}$$
28)
$$\begin{array}{r} 2 \\ \times\ 6 \\ \hline \end{array}$$
29)
$$\begin{array}{r} 1 \\ \times\ 6 \\ \hline \end{array}$$
30)
$$\begin{array}{r} 2 \\ \times\ 6 \\ \hline \end{array}$$

31)
$$\begin{array}{r} 6 \\ \times\ 4 \\ \hline \end{array}$$
32)
$$\begin{array}{r} 9 \\ \times\ 6 \\ \hline \end{array}$$
33)
$$\begin{array}{r} 6 \\ \times\ 8 \\ \hline \end{array}$$
34)
$$\begin{array}{r} 6 \\ \times\ 6 \\ \hline \end{array}$$
35)
$$\begin{array}{r} 3 \\ \times\ 6 \\ \hline \end{array}$$

Let's Multiply 6

1) $6 \times 1 = \boxed{}$ 2) $2 \times 6 = \boxed{}$ 3) $3 \times 6 = \boxed{}$

4) $1 \times 6 = \boxed{}$ 5) $7 \times 6 = \boxed{}$ 6) $6 \times 3 = \boxed{}$

7) $9 \times 6 = \boxed{}$ 8) $6 \times 3 = \boxed{}$ 9) $0 \times 6 = \boxed{}$

10) $6 \times 4 = \boxed{}$ 11) $3 \times 6 = \boxed{}$ 12) $8 \times 6 = \boxed{}$

13) $7 \times 6 = \boxed{}$ 14) $6 \times 5 = \boxed{}$ 15) $6 \times 0 = \boxed{}$

16) $\begin{array}{r} 6 \\ \times\ 8 \\ \hline \end{array}$ 17) $\begin{array}{r} 6 \\ \times\ 1 \\ \hline \end{array}$ 18) $\begin{array}{r} 9 \\ \times\ 6 \\ \hline \end{array}$ 19) $\begin{array}{r} 9 \\ \times\ 6 \\ \hline \end{array}$ 20) $\begin{array}{r} 6 \\ \times\ 6 \\ \hline \end{array}$

21) $\begin{array}{r} 0 \\ \times\ 6 \\ \hline \end{array}$ 22) $\begin{array}{r} 4 \\ \times\ 6 \\ \hline \end{array}$ 23) $\begin{array}{r} 6 \\ \times\ 3 \\ \hline \end{array}$ 24) $\begin{array}{r} 6 \\ \times\ 1 \\ \hline \end{array}$ 25) $\begin{array}{r} 9 \\ \times\ 6 \\ \hline \end{array}$

26) $\begin{array}{r} 3 \\ \times\ 6 \\ \hline \end{array}$ 27) $\begin{array}{r} 6 \\ \times\ 7 \\ \hline \end{array}$ 28) $\begin{array}{r} 6 \\ \times\ 0 \\ \hline \end{array}$ 29) $\begin{array}{r} 2 \\ \times\ 6 \\ \hline \end{array}$ 30) $\begin{array}{r} 6 \\ \times\ 9 \\ \hline \end{array}$

31) $\begin{array}{r} 0 \\ \times\ 6 \\ \hline \end{array}$ 32) $\begin{array}{r} 7 \\ \times\ 6 \\ \hline \end{array}$ 33) $\begin{array}{r} 8 \\ \times\ 6 \\ \hline \end{array}$ 34) $\begin{array}{r} 6 \\ \times\ 6 \\ \hline \end{array}$ 35) $\begin{array}{r} 6 \\ \times\ 3 \\ \hline \end{array}$

Let's Multiply 6

1) $6 \times 3 = \boxed{}$ 2) $0 \times 6 = \boxed{}$ 3) $1 \times 6 = \boxed{}$

4) $0 \times 6 = \boxed{}$ 5) $8 \times 6 = \boxed{}$ 6) $6 \times 8 = \boxed{}$

7) $9 \times 6 = \boxed{}$ 8) $6 \times 6 = \boxed{}$ 9) $4 \times 6 = \boxed{}$

10) $1 \times 6 = \boxed{}$ 11) $6 \times 1 = \boxed{}$ 12) $6 \times 4 = \boxed{}$

13) $6 \times 0 = \boxed{}$ 14) $5 \times 6 = \boxed{}$ 15) $6 \times 9 = \boxed{}$

16) 9×6 17) 7×6 18) 6×7 19) 7×6 20) 6×9

21) 2×6 22) 2×6 23) 6×2 24) 6×7 25) 1×6

26) 4×6 27) 2×6 28) 7×6 29) 6×6 30) 9×6

31) 3×6 32) 7×6 33) 6×6 34) 6×3 35) 6×6

Let's Multiply 7

1) $7 \times 0 =$ ☐ 2) $7 \times 8 =$ ☐ 3) $7 \times 1 =$ ☐

4) $3 \times 7 =$ ☐ 5) $7 \times 9 =$ ☐ 6) $7 \times 3 =$ ☐

7) $1 \times 7 =$ ☐ 8) $5 \times 7 =$ ☐ 9) $9 \times 7 =$ ☐

10) $7 \times 1 =$ ☐ 11) $7 \times 8 =$ ☐ 12) $8 \times 7 =$ ☐

13) $9 \times 7 =$ ☐ 14) $7 \times 7 =$ ☐ 15) $5 \times 7 =$ ☐

16)
$$\begin{array}{r} 0 \\ \times\ 7 \\ \hline \end{array}$$

17)
$$\begin{array}{r} 1 \\ \times\ 7 \\ \hline \end{array}$$

18)
$$\begin{array}{r} 9 \\ \times\ 7 \\ \hline \end{array}$$

19)
$$\begin{array}{r} 5 \\ \times\ 7 \\ \hline \end{array}$$

20)
$$\begin{array}{r} 4 \\ \times\ 7 \\ \hline \end{array}$$

21)
$$\begin{array}{r} 7 \\ \times\ 0 \\ \hline \end{array}$$

22)
$$\begin{array}{r} 7 \\ \times\ 9 \\ \hline \end{array}$$

23)
$$\begin{array}{r} 7 \\ \times\ 1 \\ \hline \end{array}$$

24)
$$\begin{array}{r} 7 \\ \times\ 7 \\ \hline \end{array}$$

25)
$$\begin{array}{r} 7 \\ \times\ 9 \\ \hline \end{array}$$

26)
$$\begin{array}{r} 3 \\ \times\ 7 \\ \hline \end{array}$$

27)
$$\begin{array}{r} 8 \\ \times\ 7 \\ \hline \end{array}$$

28)
$$\begin{array}{r} 9 \\ \times\ 7 \\ \hline \end{array}$$

29)
$$\begin{array}{r} 4 \\ \times\ 7 \\ \hline \end{array}$$

30)
$$\begin{array}{r} 4 \\ \times\ 7 \\ \hline \end{array}$$

31)
$$\begin{array}{r} 7 \\ \times\ 7 \\ \hline \end{array}$$

32)
$$\begin{array}{r} 7 \\ \times\ 3 \\ \hline \end{array}$$

33)
$$\begin{array}{r} 8 \\ \times\ 7 \\ \hline \end{array}$$

34)
$$\begin{array}{r} 0 \\ \times\ 7 \\ \hline \end{array}$$

35)
$$\begin{array}{r} 6 \\ \times\ 7 \\ \hline \end{array}$$

Let's Multiply 7

1) $7 \times 1 =$ ☐   2) $6 \times 7 =$ ☐   3) $7 \times 7 =$ ☐

4) $9 \times 7 =$ ☐   5) $7 \times 6 =$ ☐   6) $4 \times 7 =$ ☐

7) $8 \times 7 =$ ☐   8) $6 \times 7 =$ ☐   9) $7 \times 4 =$ ☐

10) $1 \times 7 =$ ☐   11) $7 \times 2 =$ ☐   12) $5 \times 7 =$ ☐

13) $7 \times 1 =$ ☐   14) $7 \times 7 =$ ☐   15) $7 \times 7 =$ ☐

16) $\begin{array}{r} 7 \\ \times\ 2 \\ \hline \end{array}$ 17) $\begin{array}{r} 7 \\ \times\ 7 \\ \hline \end{array}$ 18) $\begin{array}{r} 3 \\ \times\ 7 \\ \hline \end{array}$ 19) $\begin{array}{r} 7 \\ \times\ 4 \\ \hline \end{array}$ 20) $\begin{array}{r} 7 \\ \times\ 3 \\ \hline \end{array}$

21) $\begin{array}{r} 5 \\ \times\ 7 \\ \hline \end{array}$ 22) $\begin{array}{r} 7 \\ \times\ 3 \\ \hline \end{array}$ 23) $\begin{array}{r} 8 \\ \times\ 7 \\ \hline \end{array}$ 24) $\begin{array}{r} 5 \\ \times\ 7 \\ \hline \end{array}$ 25) $\begin{array}{r} 7 \\ \times\ 2 \\ \hline \end{array}$

26) $\begin{array}{r} 7 \\ \times\ 0 \\ \hline \end{array}$ 27) $\begin{array}{r} 1 \\ \times\ 7 \\ \hline \end{array}$ 28) $\begin{array}{r} 7 \\ \times\ 3 \\ \hline \end{array}$ 29) $\begin{array}{r} 4 \\ \times\ 7 \\ \hline \end{array}$ 30) $\begin{array}{r} 7 \\ \times\ 3 \\ \hline \end{array}$

31) $\begin{array}{r} 9 \\ \times\ 7 \\ \hline \end{array}$ 32) $\begin{array}{r} 2 \\ \times\ 7 \\ \hline \end{array}$ 33) $\begin{array}{r} 7 \\ \times\ 8 \\ \hline \end{array}$ 34) $\begin{array}{r} 7 \\ \times\ 0 \\ \hline \end{array}$ 35) $\begin{array}{r} 1 \\ \times\ 7 \\ \hline \end{array}$

Let's Multiply 7

1) $7 \times 7 =$ ☐ 2) $7 \times 0 =$ ☐ 3) $7 \times 7 =$ ☐

4) $7 \times 1 =$ ☐ 5) $9 \times 7 =$ ☐ 6) $3 \times 7 =$ ☐

7) $7 \times 4 =$ ☐ 8) $2 \times 7 =$ ☐ 9) $4 \times 7 =$ ☐

10) $7 \times 0 =$ ☐ 11) $7 \times 9 =$ ☐ 12) $7 \times 7 =$ ☐

13) $7 \times 6 =$ ☐ 14) $7 \times 1 =$ ☐ 15) $7 \times 5 =$ ☐

16) $\begin{array}{r} 9 \\ \times\ 7 \\ \hline \end{array}$ 17) $\begin{array}{r} 7 \\ \times\ 0 \\ \hline \end{array}$ 18) $\begin{array}{r} 6 \\ \times\ 7 \\ \hline \end{array}$ 19) $\begin{array}{r} 7 \\ \times\ 8 \\ \hline \end{array}$ 20) $\begin{array}{r} 7 \\ \times\ 7 \\ \hline \end{array}$

21) $\begin{array}{r} 5 \\ \times\ 7 \\ \hline \end{array}$ 22) $\begin{array}{r} 7 \\ \times\ 5 \\ \hline \end{array}$ 23) $\begin{array}{r} 7 \\ \times\ 1 \\ \hline \end{array}$ 24) $\begin{array}{r} 9 \\ \times\ 7 \\ \hline \end{array}$ 25) $\begin{array}{r} 7 \\ \times\ 3 \\ \hline \end{array}$

26) $\begin{array}{r} 7 \\ \times\ 4 \\ \hline \end{array}$ 27) $\begin{array}{r} 7 \\ \times\ 3 \\ \hline \end{array}$ 28) $\begin{array}{r} 7 \\ \times\ 1 \\ \hline \end{array}$ 29) $\begin{array}{r} 7 \\ \times\ 0 \\ \hline \end{array}$ 30) $\begin{array}{r} 8 \\ \times\ 7 \\ \hline \end{array}$

31) $\begin{array}{r} 5 \\ \times\ 7 \\ \hline \end{array}$ 32) $\begin{array}{r} 2 \\ \times\ 7 \\ \hline \end{array}$ 33) $\begin{array}{r} 5 \\ \times\ 7 \\ \hline \end{array}$ 34) $\begin{array}{r} 7 \\ \times\ 6 \\ \hline \end{array}$ 35) $\begin{array}{r} 0 \\ \times\ 7 \\ \hline \end{array}$

Let's Multiply 7

1) $7 \times 6 =$ ☐   2) $9 \times 7 =$ ☐   3) $7 \times 4 =$ ☐

4) $9 \times 7 =$ ☐   5) $1 \times 7 =$ ☐   6) $7 \times 0 =$ ☐

7) $5 \times 7 =$ ☐   8) $3 \times 7 =$ ☐   9) $0 \times 7 =$ ☐

10) $2 \times 7 =$ ☐   11) $5 \times 7 =$ ☐   12) $7 \times 5 =$ ☐

13) $7 \times 9 =$ ☐   14) $7 \times 7 =$ ☐   15) $7 \times 4 =$ ☐

16) $\begin{array}{r} 7 \\ \times\ 8 \\ \hline \end{array}$ 17) $\begin{array}{r} 7 \\ \times\ 1 \\ \hline \end{array}$ 18) $\begin{array}{r} 7 \\ \times\ 9 \\ \hline \end{array}$ 19) $\begin{array}{r} 5 \\ \times\ 7 \\ \hline \end{array}$ 20) $\begin{array}{r} 1 \\ \times\ 7 \\ \hline \end{array}$

21) $\begin{array}{r} 3 \\ \times\ 7 \\ \hline \end{array}$ 22) $\begin{array}{r} 6 \\ \times\ 7 \\ \hline \end{array}$ 23) $\begin{array}{r} 4 \\ \times\ 7 \\ \hline \end{array}$ 24) $\begin{array}{r} 7 \\ \times\ 1 \\ \hline \end{array}$ 25) $\begin{array}{r} 7 \\ \times\ 7 \\ \hline \end{array}$

26) $\begin{array}{r} 7 \\ \times\ 1 \\ \hline \end{array}$ 27) $\begin{array}{r} 7 \\ \times\ 4 \\ \hline \end{array}$ 28) $\begin{array}{r} 7 \\ \times\ 8 \\ \hline \end{array}$ 29) $\begin{array}{r} 7 \\ \times\ 7 \\ \hline \end{array}$ 30) $\begin{array}{r} 6 \\ \times\ 7 \\ \hline \end{array}$

31) $\begin{array}{r} 7 \\ \times\ 2 \\ \hline \end{array}$ 32) $\begin{array}{r} 7 \\ \times\ 6 \\ \hline \end{array}$ 33) $\begin{array}{r} 4 \\ \times\ 7 \\ \hline \end{array}$ 34) $\begin{array}{r} 7 \\ \times\ 5 \\ \hline \end{array}$ 35) $\begin{array}{r} 7 \\ \times\ 0 \\ \hline \end{array}$

Let's Multiply 8

1) $8 \times 3 =$ [ ]   2) $7 \times 8 =$ [ ]   3) $4 \times 8 =$ [ ]

4) $8 \times 4 =$ [ ]   5) $8 \times 1 =$ [ ]   6) $8 \times 2 =$ [ ]

7) $8 \times 8 =$ [ ]   8) $8 \times 1 =$ [ ]   9) $8 \times 5 =$ [ ]

10) $8 \times 8 =$ [ ]   11) $0 \times 8 =$ [ ]   12) $5 \times 8 =$ [ ]

13) $5 \times 8 =$ [ ]   14) $9 \times 8 =$ [ ]   15) $8 \times 5 =$ [ ]

16) $\begin{array}{r} 1 \\ \times\ 8 \\ \hline \end{array}$
17) $\begin{array}{r} 8 \\ \times\ 1 \\ \hline \end{array}$
18) $\begin{array}{r} 2 \\ \times\ 8 \\ \hline \end{array}$
19) $\begin{array}{r} 8 \\ \times\ 8 \\ \hline \end{array}$
20) $\begin{array}{r} 8 \\ \times\ 0 \\ \hline \end{array}$

21) $\begin{array}{r} 3 \\ \times\ 8 \\ \hline \end{array}$
22) $\begin{array}{r} 8 \\ \times\ 8 \\ \hline \end{array}$
23) $\begin{array}{r} 4 \\ \times\ 8 \\ \hline \end{array}$
24) $\begin{array}{r} 2 \\ \times\ 8 \\ \hline \end{array}$
25) $\begin{array}{r} 8 \\ \times\ 5 \\ \hline \end{array}$

26) $\begin{array}{r} 3 \\ \times\ 8 \\ \hline \end{array}$
27) $\begin{array}{r} 8 \\ \times\ 7 \\ \hline \end{array}$
28) $\begin{array}{r} 4 \\ \times\ 8 \\ \hline \end{array}$
29) $\begin{array}{r} 8 \\ \times\ 8 \\ \hline \end{array}$
30) $\begin{array}{r} 8 \\ \times\ 7 \\ \hline \end{array}$

31) $\begin{array}{r} 8 \\ \times\ 0 \\ \hline \end{array}$
32) $\begin{array}{r} 9 \\ \times\ 8 \\ \hline \end{array}$
33) $\begin{array}{r} 4 \\ \times\ 8 \\ \hline \end{array}$
34) $\begin{array}{r} 8 \\ \times\ 2 \\ \hline \end{array}$
35) $\begin{array}{r} 3 \\ \times\ 8 \\ \hline \end{array}$

Let's Multiply 8

1) $1 \times 8 = \boxed{}$ 2) $7 \times 8 = \boxed{}$ 3) $8 \times 7 = \boxed{}$

4) $4 \times 8 = \boxed{}$ 5) $8 \times 1 = \boxed{}$ 6) $8 \times 0 = \boxed{}$

7) $8 \times 0 = \boxed{}$ 8) $7 \times 8 = \boxed{}$ 9) $8 \times 9 = \boxed{}$

10) $4 \times 8 = \boxed{}$ 11) $8 \times 3 = \boxed{}$ 12) $1 \times 8 = \boxed{}$

13) $4 \times 8 = \boxed{}$ 14) $8 \times 4 = \boxed{}$ 15) $1 \times 8 = \boxed{}$

16) $\begin{array}{r} 8 \\ \times\ 4 \\ \hline \end{array}$ 17) $\begin{array}{r} 8 \\ \times\ 8 \\ \hline \end{array}$ 18) $\begin{array}{r} 5 \\ \times\ 8 \\ \hline \end{array}$ 19) $\begin{array}{r} 8 \\ \times\ 5 \\ \hline \end{array}$ 20) $\begin{array}{r} 8 \\ \times\ 1 \\ \hline \end{array}$

21) $\begin{array}{r} 2 \\ \times\ 8 \\ \hline \end{array}$ 22) $\begin{array}{r} 1 \\ \times\ 8 \\ \hline \end{array}$ 23) $\begin{array}{r} 9 \\ \times\ 8 \\ \hline \end{array}$ 24) $\begin{array}{r} 8 \\ \times\ 6 \\ \hline \end{array}$ 25) $\begin{array}{r} 6 \\ \times\ 8 \\ \hline \end{array}$

26) $\begin{array}{r} 8 \\ \times\ 5 \\ \hline \end{array}$ 27) $\begin{array}{r} 6 \\ \times\ 8 \\ \hline \end{array}$ 28) $\begin{array}{r} 8 \\ \times\ 0 \\ \hline \end{array}$ 29) $\begin{array}{r} 0 \\ \times\ 8 \\ \hline \end{array}$ 30) $\begin{array}{r} 9 \\ \times\ 8 \\ \hline \end{array}$

31) $\begin{array}{r} 3 \\ \times\ 8 \\ \hline \end{array}$ 32) $\begin{array}{r} 3 \\ \times\ 8 \\ \hline \end{array}$ 33) $\begin{array}{r} 8 \\ \times\ 7 \\ \hline \end{array}$ 34) $\begin{array}{r} 7 \\ \times\ 8 \\ \hline \end{array}$ 35) $\begin{array}{r} 6 \\ \times\ 8 \\ \hline \end{array}$

Let's Multiply 8

1) $9 \times 8 = \boxed{}$ 2) $6 \times 8 = \boxed{}$ 3) $8 \times 2 = \boxed{}$

4) $8 \times 3 = \boxed{}$ 5) $5 \times 8 = \boxed{}$ 6) $8 \times 6 = \boxed{}$

7) $8 \times 3 = \boxed{}$ 8) $2 \times 8 = \boxed{}$ 9) $8 \times 6 = \boxed{}$

10) $8 \times 7 = \boxed{}$ 11) $6 \times 8 = \boxed{}$ 12) $8 \times 2 = \boxed{}$

13) $3 \times 8 = \boxed{}$ 14) $8 \times 0 = \boxed{}$ 15) $8 \times 5 = \boxed{}$

16) $\begin{array}{r} 8 \\ \times\ 0 \\ \hline \end{array}$ 17) $\begin{array}{r} 0 \\ \times\ 8 \\ \hline \end{array}$ 18) $\begin{array}{r} 8 \\ \times\ 8 \\ \hline \end{array}$ 19) $\begin{array}{r} 4 \\ \times\ 8 \\ \hline \end{array}$ 20) $\begin{array}{r} 5 \\ \times\ 8 \\ \hline \end{array}$

21) $\begin{array}{r} 8 \\ \times\ 2 \\ \hline \end{array}$ 22) $\begin{array}{r} 8 \\ \times\ 2 \\ \hline \end{array}$ 23) $\begin{array}{r} 8 \\ \times\ 8 \\ \hline \end{array}$ 24) $\begin{array}{r} 4 \\ \times\ 8 \\ \hline \end{array}$ 25) $\begin{array}{r} 8 \\ \times\ 9 \\ \hline \end{array}$

26) $\begin{array}{r} 8 \\ \times\ 1 \\ \hline \end{array}$ 27) $\begin{array}{r} 5 \\ \times\ 8 \\ \hline \end{array}$ 28) $\begin{array}{r} 0 \\ \times\ 8 \\ \hline \end{array}$ 29) $\begin{array}{r} 1 \\ \times\ 8 \\ \hline \end{array}$ 30) $\begin{array}{r} 7 \\ \times\ 8 \\ \hline \end{array}$

31) $\begin{array}{r} 8 \\ \times\ 9 \\ \hline \end{array}$ 32) $\begin{array}{r} 9 \\ \times\ 8 \\ \hline \end{array}$ 33) $\begin{array}{r} 0 \\ \times\ 8 \\ \hline \end{array}$ 34) $\begin{array}{r} 3 \\ \times\ 8 \\ \hline \end{array}$ 35) $\begin{array}{r} 6 \\ \times\ 8 \\ \hline \end{array}$

Let's Multiply 8

1) $8 \times 2 =$ ☐   2) $9 \times 8 =$ ☐   3) $8 \times 2 =$ ☐

4) $8 \times 7 =$ ☐   5) $8 \times 8 =$ ☐   6) $8 \times 9 =$ ☐

7) $1 \times 8 =$ ☐   8) $2 \times 8 =$ ☐   9) $8 \times 8 =$ ☐

10) $4 \times 8 =$ ☐   11) $4 \times 8 =$ ☐   12) $6 \times 8 =$ ☐

13) $8 \times 0 =$ ☐   14) $7 \times 8 =$ ☐   15) $8 \times 8 =$ ☐

16) $\begin{array}{r} 1 \\ \times\ 8 \\ \hline \end{array}$ 17) $\begin{array}{r} 8 \\ \times\ 8 \\ \hline \end{array}$ 18) $\begin{array}{r} 8 \\ \times\ 3 \\ \hline \end{array}$ 19) $\begin{array}{r} 8 \\ \times\ 1 \\ \hline \end{array}$ 20) $\begin{array}{r} 5 \\ \times\ 8 \\ \hline \end{array}$

21) $\begin{array}{r} 7 \\ \times\ 8 \\ \hline \end{array}$ 22) $\begin{array}{r} 8 \\ \times\ 9 \\ \hline \end{array}$ 23) $\begin{array}{r} 1 \\ \times\ 8 \\ \hline \end{array}$ 24) $\begin{array}{r} 6 \\ \times\ 8 \\ \hline \end{array}$ 25) $\begin{array}{r} 8 \\ \times\ 8 \\ \hline \end{array}$

26) $\begin{array}{r} 4 \\ \times\ 8 \\ \hline \end{array}$ 27) $\begin{array}{r} 7 \\ \times\ 8 \\ \hline \end{array}$ 28) $\begin{array}{r} 2 \\ \times\ 8 \\ \hline \end{array}$ 29) $\begin{array}{r} 1 \\ \times\ 8 \\ \hline \end{array}$ 30) $\begin{array}{r} 8 \\ \times\ 6 \\ \hline \end{array}$

31) $\begin{array}{r} 3 \\ \times\ 8 \\ \hline \end{array}$ 32) $\begin{array}{r} 8 \\ \times\ 0 \\ \hline \end{array}$ 33) $\begin{array}{r} 3 \\ \times\ 8 \\ \hline \end{array}$ 34) $\begin{array}{r} 8 \\ \times\ 7 \\ \hline \end{array}$ 35) $\begin{array}{r} 8 \\ \times\ 0 \\ \hline \end{array}$

Let's Multiply 9

1) $9 \times 9 = \boxed{}$ 2) $3 \times 9 = \boxed{}$ 3) $9 \times 5 = \boxed{}$

4) $9 \times 4 = \boxed{}$ 5) $9 \times 5 = \boxed{}$ 6) $9 \times 1 = \boxed{}$

7) $0 \times 9 = \boxed{}$ 8) $3 \times 9 = \boxed{}$ 9) $5 \times 9 = \boxed{}$

10) $9 \times 9 = \boxed{}$ 11) $9 \times 2 = \boxed{}$ 12) $9 \times 1 = \boxed{}$

13) $9 \times 7 = \boxed{}$ 14) $3 \times 9 = \boxed{}$ 15) $9 \times 4 = \boxed{}$

16)
$$\begin{array}{r} 4 \\ \times\ 9 \\ \hline \end{array}$$

17)
$$\begin{array}{r} 6 \\ \times\ 9 \\ \hline \end{array}$$

18)
$$\begin{array}{r} 7 \\ \times\ 9 \\ \hline \end{array}$$

19)
$$\begin{array}{r} 5 \\ \times\ 9 \\ \hline \end{array}$$

20)
$$\begin{array}{r} 9 \\ \times\ 7 \\ \hline \end{array}$$

21)
$$\begin{array}{r} 9 \\ \times\ 0 \\ \hline \end{array}$$

22)
$$\begin{array}{r} 2 \\ \times\ 9 \\ \hline \end{array}$$

23)
$$\begin{array}{r} 9 \\ \times\ 8 \\ \hline \end{array}$$

24)
$$\begin{array}{r} 8 \\ \times\ 9 \\ \hline \end{array}$$

25)
$$\begin{array}{r} 1 \\ \times\ 9 \\ \hline \end{array}$$

26)
$$\begin{array}{r} 9 \\ \times\ 9 \\ \hline \end{array}$$

27)
$$\begin{array}{r} 6 \\ \times\ 9 \\ \hline \end{array}$$

28)
$$\begin{array}{r} 5 \\ \times\ 9 \\ \hline \end{array}$$

29)
$$\begin{array}{r} 9 \\ \times\ 8 \\ \hline \end{array}$$

30)
$$\begin{array}{r} 5 \\ \times\ 9 \\ \hline \end{array}$$

31)
$$\begin{array}{r} 9 \\ \times\ 1 \\ \hline \end{array}$$

32)
$$\begin{array}{r} 9 \\ \times\ 4 \\ \hline \end{array}$$

33)
$$\begin{array}{r} 9 \\ \times\ 4 \\ \hline \end{array}$$

34)
$$\begin{array}{r} 2 \\ \times\ 9 \\ \hline \end{array}$$

35)
$$\begin{array}{r} 9 \\ \times\ 2 \\ \hline \end{array}$$

Let's Multiply 9

1) $5 \times 9 =$ ☐   2) $9 \times 2 =$ ☐   3) $9 \times 3 =$ ☐

4) $2 \times 9 =$ ☐   5) $9 \times 1 =$ ☐   6) $9 \times 6 =$ ☐

7) $9 \times 7 =$ ☐   8) $9 \times 6 =$ ☐   9) $1 \times 9 =$ ☐

10) $9 \times 4 =$ ☐   11) $0 \times 9 =$ ☐   12) $9 \times 6 =$ ☐

13) $1 \times 9 =$ ☐   14) $9 \times 0 =$ ☐   15) $6 \times 9 =$ ☐

16)
$$\begin{array}{r} 4 \\ \times\ 9 \\ \hline \end{array}$$

17)
$$\begin{array}{r} 9 \\ \times\ 1 \\ \hline \end{array}$$

18)
$$\begin{array}{r} 3 \\ \times\ 9 \\ \hline \end{array}$$

19)
$$\begin{array}{r} 9 \\ \times\ 8 \\ \hline \end{array}$$

20)
$$\begin{array}{r} 5 \\ \times\ 9 \\ \hline \end{array}$$

21)
$$\begin{array}{r} 7 \\ \times\ 9 \\ \hline \end{array}$$

22)
$$\begin{array}{r} 9 \\ \times\ 2 \\ \hline \end{array}$$

23)
$$\begin{array}{r} 7 \\ \times\ 9 \\ \hline \end{array}$$

24)
$$\begin{array}{r} 9 \\ \times\ 3 \\ \hline \end{array}$$

25)
$$\begin{array}{r} 9 \\ \times\ 6 \\ \hline \end{array}$$

26)
$$\begin{array}{r} 9 \\ \times\ 9 \\ \hline \end{array}$$

27)
$$\begin{array}{r} 6 \\ \times\ 9 \\ \hline \end{array}$$

28)
$$\begin{array}{r} 7 \\ \times\ 9 \\ \hline \end{array}$$

29)
$$\begin{array}{r} 3 \\ \times\ 9 \\ \hline \end{array}$$

30)
$$\begin{array}{r} 9 \\ \times\ 8 \\ \hline \end{array}$$

31)
$$\begin{array}{r} 5 \\ \times\ 9 \\ \hline \end{array}$$

32)
$$\begin{array}{r} 1 \\ \times\ 9 \\ \hline \end{array}$$

33)
$$\begin{array}{r} 9 \\ \times\ 3 \\ \hline \end{array}$$

34)
$$\begin{array}{r} 9 \\ \times\ 0 \\ \hline \end{array}$$

35)
$$\begin{array}{r} 2 \\ \times\ 9 \\ \hline \end{array}$$

Let's Multiply 9

1) $8 \times 9 =$ ☐   2) $9 \times 7 =$ ☐   3) $7 \times 9 =$ ☐

4) $9 \times 0 =$ ☐   5) $9 \times 2 =$ ☐   6) $9 \times 4 =$ ☐

7) $8 \times 9 =$ ☐   8) $9 \times 9 =$ ☐   9) $9 \times 4 =$ ☐

10) $5 \times 9 =$ ☐   11) $9 \times 8 =$ ☐   12) $2 \times 9 =$ ☐

13) $9 \times 9 =$ ☐   14) $8 \times 9 =$ ☐   15) $3 \times 9 =$ ☐

16) $\begin{array}{r} 1 \\ \times\ 9 \\ \hline \end{array}$ 17) $\begin{array}{r} 9 \\ \times\ 1 \\ \hline \end{array}$ 18) $\begin{array}{r} 9 \\ \times\ 3 \\ \hline \end{array}$ 19) $\begin{array}{r} 9 \\ \times\ 9 \\ \hline \end{array}$ 20) $\begin{array}{r} 9 \\ \times\ 2 \\ \hline \end{array}$

21) $\begin{array}{r} 0 \\ \times\ 9 \\ \hline \end{array}$ 22) $\begin{array}{r} 9 \\ \times\ 3 \\ \hline \end{array}$ 23) $\begin{array}{r} 2 \\ \times\ 9 \\ \hline \end{array}$ 24) $\begin{array}{r} 0 \\ \times\ 9 \\ \hline \end{array}$ 25) $\begin{array}{r} 7 \\ \times\ 9 \\ \hline \end{array}$

26) $\begin{array}{r} 8 \\ \times\ 9 \\ \hline \end{array}$ 27) $\begin{array}{r} 9 \\ \times\ 5 \\ \hline \end{array}$ 28) $\begin{array}{r} 9 \\ \times\ 0 \\ \hline \end{array}$ 29) $\begin{array}{r} 6 \\ \times\ 9 \\ \hline \end{array}$ 30) $\begin{array}{r} 0 \\ \times\ 9 \\ \hline \end{array}$

31) $\begin{array}{r} 9 \\ \times\ 2 \\ \hline \end{array}$ 32) $\begin{array}{r} 9 \\ \times\ 3 \\ \hline \end{array}$ 33) $\begin{array}{r} 7 \\ \times\ 9 \\ \hline \end{array}$ 34) $\begin{array}{r} 9 \\ \times\ 5 \\ \hline \end{array}$ 35) $\begin{array}{r} 6 \\ \times\ 9 \\ \hline \end{array}$

Let's Multiply 9

1) $9 \times 6 = \boxed{}$ 2) $9 \times 7 = \boxed{}$ 3) $3 \times 9 = \boxed{}$

4) $2 \times 9 = \boxed{}$ 5) $3 \times 9 = \boxed{}$ 6) $9 \times 8 = \boxed{}$

7) $3 \times 9 = \boxed{}$ 8) $5 \times 9 = \boxed{}$ 9) $6 \times 9 = \boxed{}$

10) $9 \times 6 = \boxed{}$ 11) $8 \times 9 = \boxed{}$ 12) $0 \times 9 = \boxed{}$

13) $9 \times 0 = \boxed{}$ 14) $4 \times 9 = \boxed{}$ 15) $9 \times 6 = \boxed{}$

16) $\begin{array}{r} 8 \\ \times\ 9 \\ \hline \end{array}$ 17) $\begin{array}{r} 9 \\ \times\ 6 \\ \hline \end{array}$ 18) $\begin{array}{r} 4 \\ \times\ 9 \\ \hline \end{array}$ 19) $\begin{array}{r} 9 \\ \times\ 6 \\ \hline \end{array}$ 20) $\begin{array}{r} 9 \\ \times\ 1 \\ \hline \end{array}$

21) $\begin{array}{r} 4 \\ \times\ 9 \\ \hline \end{array}$ 22) $\begin{array}{r} 9 \\ \times\ 2 \\ \hline \end{array}$ 23) $\begin{array}{r} 5 \\ \times\ 9 \\ \hline \end{array}$ 24) $\begin{array}{r} 2 \\ \times\ 9 \\ \hline \end{array}$ 25) $\begin{array}{r} 2 \\ \times\ 9 \\ \hline \end{array}$

26) $\begin{array}{r} 9 \\ \times\ 9 \\ \hline \end{array}$ 27) $\begin{array}{r} 2 \\ \times\ 9 \\ \hline \end{array}$ 28) $\begin{array}{r} 1 \\ \times\ 9 \\ \hline \end{array}$ 29) $\begin{array}{r} 8 \\ \times\ 9 \\ \hline \end{array}$ 30) $\begin{array}{r} 8 \\ \times\ 9 \\ \hline \end{array}$

31) $\begin{array}{r} 6 \\ \times\ 9 \\ \hline \end{array}$ 32) $\begin{array}{r} 9 \\ \times\ 5 \\ \hline \end{array}$ 33) $\begin{array}{r} 9 \\ \times\ 0 \\ \hline \end{array}$ 34) $\begin{array}{r} 3 \\ \times\ 9 \\ \hline \end{array}$ 35) $\begin{array}{r} 2 \\ \times\ 9 \\ \hline \end{array}$

Let's Multiply 10

1) $10 \times 9 = \boxed{}$ 2) $9 \times 10 = \boxed{}$ 3) $5 \times 10 = \boxed{}$

4) $0 \times 10 = \boxed{}$ 5) $10 \times 2 = \boxed{}$ 6) $10 \times 3 = \boxed{}$

7) $6 \times 10 = \boxed{}$ 8) $10 \times 7 = \boxed{}$ 9) $10 \times 9 = \boxed{}$

10) $10 \times 6 = \boxed{}$ 11) $10 \times 8 = \boxed{}$ 12) $6 \times 10 = \boxed{}$

13) $10 \times 1 = \boxed{}$ 14) $0 \times 10 = \boxed{}$ 15) $10 \times 5 = \boxed{}$

16) $\begin{array}{r} 10 \\ \times\ 9 \\ \hline \end{array}$ 17) $\begin{array}{r} 2 \\ \times\ 10 \\ \hline \end{array}$ 18) $\begin{array}{r} 3 \\ \times\ 10 \\ \hline \end{array}$ 19) $\begin{array}{r} 10 \\ \times\ 1 \\ \hline \end{array}$ 20) $\begin{array}{r} 8 \\ \times\ 10 \\ \hline \end{array}$

21) $\begin{array}{r} 10 \\ \times\ 4 \\ \hline \end{array}$ 22) $\begin{array}{r} 3 \\ \times\ 10 \\ \hline \end{array}$ 23) $\begin{array}{r} 10 \\ \times\ 3 \\ \hline \end{array}$ 24) $\begin{array}{r} 1 \\ \times\ 10 \\ \hline \end{array}$ 25) $\begin{array}{r} 10 \\ \times\ 6 \\ \hline \end{array}$

26) $\begin{array}{r} 1 \\ \times\ 10 \\ \hline \end{array}$ 27) $\begin{array}{r} 10 \\ \times\ 4 \\ \hline \end{array}$ 28) $\begin{array}{r} 6 \\ \times\ 10 \\ \hline \end{array}$ 29) $\begin{array}{r} 10 \\ \times\ 4 \\ \hline \end{array}$ 30) $\begin{array}{r} 10 \\ \times\ 6 \\ \hline \end{array}$

31) $\begin{array}{r} 10 \\ \times\ 4 \\ \hline \end{array}$ 32) $\begin{array}{r} 7 \\ \times\ 10 \\ \hline \end{array}$ 33) $\begin{array}{r} 7 \\ \times\ 10 \\ \hline \end{array}$ 34) $\begin{array}{r} 10 \\ \times\ 2 \\ \hline \end{array}$ 35) $\begin{array}{r} 0 \\ \times\ 10 \\ \hline \end{array}$

Let's Multiply 10

1) $3 \times 10 = $ [ ] 2) $10 \times 3 = $ [ ] 3) $7 \times 10 = $ [ ]

4) $10 \times 5 = $ [ ] 5) $10 \times 6 = $ [ ] 6) $10 \times 7 = $ [ ]

7) $7 \times 10 = $ [ ] 8) $10 \times 9 = $ [ ] 9) $10 \times 2 = $ [ ]

10) $10 \times 7 = $ [ ] 11) $10 \times 0 = $ [ ] 12) $4 \times 10 = $ [ ]

13) $1 \times 10 = $ [ ] 14) $10 \times 1 = $ [ ] 15) $10 \times 3 = $ [ ]

16) $\begin{array}{r} 10 \\ \times\ 7 \\ \hline \end{array}$ 17) $\begin{array}{r} 10 \\ \times\ 6 \\ \hline \end{array}$ 18) $\begin{array}{r} 1 \\ \times\ 10 \\ \hline \end{array}$ 19) $\begin{array}{r} 10 \\ \times\ 8 \\ \hline \end{array}$ 20) $\begin{array}{r} 2 \\ \times\ 10 \\ \hline \end{array}$

21) $\begin{array}{r} 2 \\ \times\ 10 \\ \hline \end{array}$ 22) $\begin{array}{r} 10 \\ \times\ 4 \\ \hline \end{array}$ 23) $\begin{array}{r} 0 \\ \times\ 10 \\ \hline \end{array}$ 24) $\begin{array}{r} 10 \\ \times\ 7 \\ \hline \end{array}$ 25) $\begin{array}{r} 3 \\ \times\ 10 \\ \hline \end{array}$

26) $\begin{array}{r} 10 \\ \times\ 3 \\ \hline \end{array}$ 27) $\begin{array}{r} 2 \\ \times\ 10 \\ \hline \end{array}$ 28) $\begin{array}{r} 1 \\ \times\ 10 \\ \hline \end{array}$ 29) $\begin{array}{r} 10 \\ \times\ 7 \\ \hline \end{array}$ 30) $\begin{array}{r} 10 \\ \times\ 6 \\ \hline \end{array}$

31) $\begin{array}{r} 6 \\ \times\ 10 \\ \hline \end{array}$ 32) $\begin{array}{r} 0 \\ \times\ 10 \\ \hline \end{array}$ 33) $\begin{array}{r} 10 \\ \times\ 6 \\ \hline \end{array}$ 34) $\begin{array}{r} 10 \\ \times\ 6 \\ \hline \end{array}$ 35) $\begin{array}{r} 3 \\ \times\ 10 \\ \hline \end{array}$

Let's Multiply 10

1) $10 \times 3 = $ ☐   2) $5 \times 10 = $ ☐   3) $10 \times 8 = $ ☐

4) $10 \times 6 = $ ☐   5) $10 \times 4 = $ ☐   6) $2 \times 10 = $ ☐

7) $10 \times 3 = $ ☐   8) $10 \times 4 = $ ☐   9) $10 \times 1 = $ ☐

10) $10 \times 0 = $ ☐   11) $6 \times 10 = $ ☐   12) $10 \times 6 = $ ☐

13) $10 \times 6 = $ ☐   14) $9 \times 10 = $ ☐   15) $10 \times 0 = $ ☐

16)
$$\begin{array}{r} 10 \\ \times\ \ 5 \\ \hline \end{array}$$

17)
$$\begin{array}{r} 4 \\ \times\ 10 \\ \hline \end{array}$$

18)
$$\begin{array}{r} 7 \\ \times\ 10 \\ \hline \end{array}$$

19)
$$\begin{array}{r} 10 \\ \times\ \ 2 \\ \hline \end{array}$$

20)
$$\begin{array}{r} 6 \\ \times\ 10 \\ \hline \end{array}$$

21)
$$\begin{array}{r} 0 \\ \times\ 10 \\ \hline \end{array}$$

22)
$$\begin{array}{r} 1 \\ \times\ 10 \\ \hline \end{array}$$

23)
$$\begin{array}{r} 2 \\ \times\ 10 \\ \hline \end{array}$$

24)
$$\begin{array}{r} 10 \\ \times\ \ 7 \\ \hline \end{array}$$

25)
$$\begin{array}{r} 5 \\ \times\ 10 \\ \hline \end{array}$$

26)
$$\begin{array}{r} 10 \\ \times\ \ 6 \\ \hline \end{array}$$

27)
$$\begin{array}{r} 0 \\ \times\ 10 \\ \hline \end{array}$$

28)
$$\begin{array}{r} 10 \\ \times\ \ 7 \\ \hline \end{array}$$

29)
$$\begin{array}{r} 7 \\ \times\ 10 \\ \hline \end{array}$$

30)
$$\begin{array}{r} 7 \\ \times\ 10 \\ \hline \end{array}$$

31)
$$\begin{array}{r} 10 \\ \times\ \ 2 \\ \hline \end{array}$$

32)
$$\begin{array}{r} 5 \\ \times\ 10 \\ \hline \end{array}$$

33)
$$\begin{array}{r} 9 \\ \times\ 10 \\ \hline \end{array}$$

34)
$$\begin{array}{r} 4 \\ \times\ 10 \\ \hline \end{array}$$

35)
$$\begin{array}{r} 3 \\ \times\ 10 \\ \hline \end{array}$$

Let's Multiply 10

1) $6 \times 10 =$ ☐   2) $10 \times 1 =$ ☐   3) $3 \times 10 =$ ☐

4) $10 \times 7 =$ ☐   5) $4 \times 10 =$ ☐   6) $2 \times 10 =$ ☐

7) $10 \times 8 =$ ☐   8) $10 \times 9 =$ ☐   9) $10 \times 5 =$ ☐

10) $6 \times 10 =$ ☐   11) $2 \times 10 =$ ☐   12) $10 \times 0 =$ ☐

13) $10 \times 7 =$ ☐   14) $0 \times 10 =$ ☐   15) $5 \times 10 =$ ☐

16)	17)	18)	19)	20)
0 × 10	9 × 10	10 × 7	6 × 10	10 × 2
☐	☐	☐	☐	☐

21)	22)	23)	24)	25)
10 × 0	10 × 2	5 × 10	10 × 0	4 × 10
☐	☐	☐	☐	☐

26)	27)	28)	29)	30)
2 × 10	10 × 8	7 × 10	10 × 6	10 × 1
☐	☐	☐	☐	☐

31)	32)	33)	34)	35)
1 × 10	10 × 5	10 × 5	10 × 0	10 × 8
☐	☐	☐	☐	☐

Let's Multiply 11 & 12

1) $2 \times 12 = $ [___] 2) $12 \times 2 = $ [___] 3) $11 \times 3 = $ [___]

4) $7 \times 12 = $ [___] 5) $11 \times 5 = $ [___] 6) $11 \times 8 = $ [___]

7) $1 \times 11 = $ [___] 8) $11 \times 9 = $ [___] 9) $12 \times 2 = $ [___]

10) $2 \times 12 = $ [___] 11) $12 \times 1 = $ [___] 12) $11 \times 4 = $ [___]

13) $0 \times 11 = $ [___] 14) $9 \times 11 = $ [___] 15) $9 \times 12 = $ [___]

16)
$$\begin{array}{r} 3 \\ \times\ 11 \\ \hline \end{array}$$
17)
$$\begin{array}{r} 0 \\ \times\ 11 \\ \hline \end{array}$$
18)
$$\begin{array}{r} 9 \\ \times\ 11 \\ \hline \end{array}$$
19)
$$\begin{array}{r} 9 \\ \times\ 11 \\ \hline \end{array}$$
20)
$$\begin{array}{r} 12 \\ \times\ 3 \\ \hline \end{array}$$

21)
$$\begin{array}{r} 1 \\ \times\ 12 \\ \hline \end{array}$$
22)
$$\begin{array}{r} 12 \\ \times\ 6 \\ \hline \end{array}$$
23)
$$\begin{array}{r} 1 \\ \times\ 11 \\ \hline \end{array}$$
24)
$$\begin{array}{r} 2 \\ \times\ 11 \\ \hline \end{array}$$
25)
$$\begin{array}{r} 4 \\ \times\ 11 \\ \hline \end{array}$$

26)
$$\begin{array}{r} 11 \\ \times\ 9 \\ \hline \end{array}$$
27)
$$\begin{array}{r} 7 \\ \times\ 11 \\ \hline \end{array}$$
28)
$$\begin{array}{r} 11 \\ \times\ 8 \\ \hline \end{array}$$
29)
$$\begin{array}{r} 5 \\ \times\ 12 \\ \hline \end{array}$$
30)
$$\begin{array}{r} 3 \\ \times\ 11 \\ \hline \end{array}$$

31)
$$\begin{array}{r} 4 \\ \times\ 11 \\ \hline \end{array}$$
32)
$$\begin{array}{r} 11 \\ \times\ 5 \\ \hline \end{array}$$
33)
$$\begin{array}{r} 12 \\ \times\ 8 \\ \hline \end{array}$$
34)
$$\begin{array}{r} 8 \\ \times\ 12 \\ \hline \end{array}$$
35)
$$\begin{array}{r} 12 \\ \times\ 3 \\ \hline \end{array}$$

Let's Multiply 11 & 12

1) $4 \times 11 = $ ☐   2) $11 \times 9 = $ ☐   3) $2 \times 12 = $ ☐

4) $12 \times 0 = $ ☐   5) $12 \times 5 = $ ☐   6) $7 \times 12 = $ ☐

7) $1 \times 11 = $ ☐   8) $11 \times 1 = $ ☐   9) $0 \times 11 = $ ☐

10) $6 \times 12 = $ ☐   11) $6 \times 11 = $ ☐   12) $12 \times 6 = $ ☐

13) $11 \times 4 = $ ☐   14) $5 \times 11 = $ ☐   15) $1 \times 12 = $ ☐

16) $\begin{array}{r} 12 \\ \times\ 3 \\ \hline \end{array}$ 17) $\begin{array}{r} 8 \\ \times\ 12 \\ \hline \end{array}$ 18) $\begin{array}{r} 11 \\ \times\ 8 \\ \hline \end{array}$ 19) $\begin{array}{r} 11 \\ \times\ 6 \\ \hline \end{array}$ 20) $\begin{array}{r} 9 \\ \times\ 11 \\ \hline \end{array}$

21) $\begin{array}{r} 12 \\ \times\ 7 \\ \hline \end{array}$ 22) $\begin{array}{r} 0 \\ \times\ 12 \\ \hline \end{array}$ 23) $\begin{array}{r} 7 \\ \times\ 11 \\ \hline \end{array}$ 24) $\begin{array}{r} 11 \\ \times\ 9 \\ \hline \end{array}$ 25) $\begin{array}{r} 11 \\ \times\ 6 \\ \hline \end{array}$

26) $\begin{array}{r} 12 \\ \times\ 6 \\ \hline \end{array}$ 27) $\begin{array}{r} 12 \\ \times\ 0 \\ \hline \end{array}$ 28) $\begin{array}{r} 3 \\ \times\ 11 \\ \hline \end{array}$ 29) $\begin{array}{r} 0 \\ \times\ 12 \\ \hline \end{array}$ 30) $\begin{array}{r} 9 \\ \times\ 11 \\ \hline \end{array}$

31) $\begin{array}{r} 4 \\ \times\ 12 \\ \hline \end{array}$ 32) $\begin{array}{r} 12 \\ \times\ 3 \\ \hline \end{array}$ 33) $\begin{array}{r} 11 \\ \times\ 7 \\ \hline \end{array}$ 34) $\begin{array}{r} 8 \\ \times\ 12 \\ \hline \end{array}$ 35) $\begin{array}{r} 2 \\ \times\ 11 \\ \hline \end{array}$

Let's Multiply 11 & 12

1) $2 \times 12 = \boxed{}$ 2) $11 \times 0 = \boxed{}$ 3) $11 \times 2 = \boxed{}$

4) $2 \times 12 = \boxed{}$ 5) $4 \times 12 = \boxed{}$ 6) $8 \times 12 = \boxed{}$

7) $11 \times 0 = \boxed{}$ 8) $12 \times 1 = \boxed{}$ 9) $7 \times 12 = \boxed{}$

10) $11 \times 2 = \boxed{}$ 11) $5 \times 11 = \boxed{}$ 12) $11 \times 7 = \boxed{}$

13) $11 \times 9 = \boxed{}$ 14) $12 \times 1 = \boxed{}$ 15) $8 \times 12 = \boxed{}$

16)
$$\begin{array}{r} 0 \\ \times\ 11 \\ \hline \end{array}$$

17)
$$\begin{array}{r} 12 \\ \times\ 8 \\ \hline \end{array}$$

18)
$$\begin{array}{r} 11 \\ \times\ 6 \\ \hline \end{array}$$

19)
$$\begin{array}{r} 1 \\ \times\ 11 \\ \hline \end{array}$$

20)
$$\begin{array}{r} 12 \\ \times\ 1 \\ \hline \end{array}$$

21)
$$\begin{array}{r} 6 \\ \times\ 11 \\ \hline \end{array}$$

22)
$$\begin{array}{r} 11 \\ \times\ 3 \\ \hline \end{array}$$

23)
$$\begin{array}{r} 8 \\ \times\ 12 \\ \hline \end{array}$$

24)
$$\begin{array}{r} 0 \\ \times\ 11 \\ \hline \end{array}$$

25)
$$\begin{array}{r} 1 \\ \times\ 11 \\ \hline \end{array}$$

26)
$$\begin{array}{r} 9 \\ \times\ 12 \\ \hline \end{array}$$

27)
$$\begin{array}{r} 1 \\ \times\ 12 \\ \hline \end{array}$$

28)
$$\begin{array}{r} 12 \\ \times\ 8 \\ \hline \end{array}$$

29)
$$\begin{array}{r} 1 \\ \times\ 12 \\ \hline \end{array}$$

30)
$$\begin{array}{r} 12 \\ \times\ 4 \\ \hline \end{array}$$

31)
$$\begin{array}{r} 12 \\ \times\ 7 \\ \hline \end{array}$$

32)
$$\begin{array}{r} 6 \\ \times\ 11 \\ \hline \end{array}$$

33)
$$\begin{array}{r} 11 \\ \times\ 5 \\ \hline \end{array}$$

34)
$$\begin{array}{r} 3 \\ \times\ 11 \\ \hline \end{array}$$

35)
$$\begin{array}{r} 12 \\ \times\ 5 \\ \hline \end{array}$$

Let's Multiply 11 & 12

1) $8 \times 12 =$ [ ] 2) $7 \times 12 =$ [ ] 3) $12 \times 8 =$ [ ]

4) $0 \times 12 =$ [ ] 5) $0 \times 11 =$ [ ] 6) $0 \times 11 =$ [ ]

7) $12 \times 4 =$ [ ] 8) $11 \times 0 =$ [ ] 9) $12 \times 1 =$ [ ]

10) $11 \times 7 =$ [ ] 11) $12 \times 6 =$ [ ] 12) $11 \times 2 =$ [ ]

13) $11 \times 6 =$ [ ] 14) $9 \times 12 =$ [ ] 15) $12 \times 2 =$ [ ]

16) $\begin{array}{r} 11 \\ \times\ 9 \\ \hline \end{array}$ 17) $\begin{array}{r} 12 \\ \times\ 0 \\ \hline \end{array}$ 18) $\begin{array}{r} 9 \\ \times\ 11 \\ \hline \end{array}$ 19) $\begin{array}{r} 12 \\ \times\ 1 \\ \hline \end{array}$ 20) $\begin{array}{r} 12 \\ \times\ 4 \\ \hline \end{array}$

21) $\begin{array}{r} 12 \\ \times\ 5 \\ \hline \end{array}$ 22) $\begin{array}{r} 12 \\ \times\ 4 \\ \hline \end{array}$ 23) $\begin{array}{r} 4 \\ \times\ 12 \\ \hline \end{array}$ 24) $\begin{array}{r} 4 \\ \times\ 11 \\ \hline \end{array}$ 25) $\begin{array}{r} 5 \\ \times\ 11 \\ \hline \end{array}$

26) $\begin{array}{r} 12 \\ \times\ 2 \\ \hline \end{array}$ 27) $\begin{array}{r} 11 \\ \times\ 9 \\ \hline \end{array}$ 28) $\begin{array}{r} 2 \\ \times\ 12 \\ \hline \end{array}$ 29) $\begin{array}{r} 2 \\ \times\ 11 \\ \hline \end{array}$ 30) $\begin{array}{r} 11 \\ \times\ 6 \\ \hline \end{array}$

31) $\begin{array}{r} 4 \\ \times\ 11 \\ \hline \end{array}$ 32) $\begin{array}{r} 11 \\ \times\ 7 \\ \hline \end{array}$ 33) $\begin{array}{r} 9 \\ \times\ 11 \\ \hline \end{array}$ 34) $\begin{array}{r} 12 \\ \times\ 3 \\ \hline \end{array}$ 35) $\begin{array}{r} 11 \\ \times\ 6 \\ \hline \end{array}$

Mixed Multiplication 0 To 12

1)
$$\begin{array}{r} 7 \\ \times\ 8 \\ \hline \end{array}$$

2)
$$\begin{array}{r} 9 \\ \times\ 2 \\ \hline \end{array}$$

3)
$$\begin{array}{r} 10 \\ \times\ 1 \\ \hline \end{array}$$

4)
$$\begin{array}{r} 0 \\ \times\ 4 \\ \hline \end{array}$$

5)
$$\begin{array}{r} 3 \\ \times\ 5 \\ \hline \end{array}$$

6)
$$\begin{array}{r} 12 \\ \times\ 1 \\ \hline \end{array}$$

7)
$$\begin{array}{r} 12 \\ \times\ 4 \\ \hline \end{array}$$

8)
$$\begin{array}{r} 3 \\ \times\ 8 \\ \hline \end{array}$$

9)
$$\begin{array}{r} 10 \\ \times\ 3 \\ \hline \end{array}$$

10)
$$\begin{array}{r} 10 \\ \times\ 6 \\ \hline \end{array}$$

11)
$$\begin{array}{r} 10 \\ \times\ 1 \\ \hline \end{array}$$

12)
$$\begin{array}{r} 11 \\ \times\ 9 \\ \hline \end{array}$$

13)
$$\begin{array}{r} 10 \\ \times\ 1 \\ \hline \end{array}$$

14)
$$\begin{array}{r} 1 \\ \times\ 8 \\ \hline \end{array}$$

15)
$$\begin{array}{r} 1 \\ \times\ 7 \\ \hline \end{array}$$

16)
$$\begin{array}{r} 10 \\ \times\ 1 \\ \hline \end{array}$$

17)
$$\begin{array}{r} 10 \\ \times\ 1 \\ \hline \end{array}$$

18)
$$\begin{array}{r} 9 \\ \times\ 3 \\ \hline \end{array}$$

19)
$$\begin{array}{r} 4 \\ \times\ 8 \\ \hline \end{array}$$

20)
$$\begin{array}{r} 11 \\ \times\ 0 \\ \hline \end{array}$$

21)
$$\begin{array}{r} 4 \\ \times\ 9 \\ \hline \end{array}$$

22)
$$\begin{array}{r} 9 \\ \times\ 7 \\ \hline \end{array}$$

23)
$$\begin{array}{r} 0 \\ \times\ 0 \\ \hline \end{array}$$

24)
$$\begin{array}{r} 10 \\ \times\ 3 \\ \hline \end{array}$$

25)
$$\begin{array}{r} 1 \\ \times\ 6 \\ \hline \end{array}$$

26)
$$\begin{array}{r} 12 \\ \times\ 1 \\ \hline \end{array}$$

27)
$$\begin{array}{r} 7 \\ \times\ 9 \\ \hline \end{array}$$

28)
$$\begin{array}{r} 10 \\ \times\ 6 \\ \hline \end{array}$$

29)
$$\begin{array}{r} 9 \\ \times\ 2 \\ \hline \end{array}$$

30)
$$\begin{array}{r} 3 \\ \times\ 1 \\ \hline \end{array}$$

31)
$$\begin{array}{r} 10 \\ \times\ 8 \\ \hline \end{array}$$

32)
$$\begin{array}{r} 10 \\ \times\ 0 \\ \hline \end{array}$$

33)
$$\begin{array}{r} 1 \\ \times\ 3 \\ \hline \end{array}$$

34)
$$\begin{array}{r} 1 \\ \times\ 6 \\ \hline \end{array}$$

35)
$$\begin{array}{r} 6 \\ \times\ 2 \\ \hline \end{array}$$

Mixed Multiplication 0 To 12

1) 12
  × 7
  ____

2)   6
  × 6
  ____

3)   3
  × 6
  ____

4) 12
  × 8
  ____

5) 12
  × 1
  ____

6)   8
  × 3
  ____

7)   6
  × 5
  ____

8)   7
  × 5
  ____

9)   6
  × 4
  ____

10)   7
  × 7
  ____

11) 12
  × 1
  ____

12)   6
  × 0
  ____

13)   9
  × 5
  ____

14)   2
  × 1
  ____

15)   4
  × 6
  ____

16)   9
  × 6
  ____

17)   5
  × 8
  ____

18)   2
  × 9
  ____

19)   5
  × 2
  ____

20)   2
  × 2
  ____

21)   2
  × 0
  ____

22)   6
  × 5
  ____

23)   5
  × 8
  ____

24)   4
  × 4
  ____

25)   2
  × 0
  ____

26)   1
  × 5
  ____

27)   0
  × 3
  ____

28) 10
  × 7
  ____

29) 10
  × 0
  ____

30) 11
  × 9
  ____

31) 10
  × 6
  ____

32)   2
  × 2
  ____

33)   3
  × 1
  ____

34)   0
  × 6
  ____

35)   7
  × 8
  ____

Mixed Multiplication 0 To 12

1) 7 × 3

2) 5 × 7

3) 3 × 9

4) 9 × 4

5) 8 × 3

6) 3 × 5

7) 1 × 8

8) 9 × 5

9) 3 × 6

10) 0 × 6

11) 8 × 2

12) 1 × 7

13) 3 × 7

14) 10 × 6

15) 8 × 4

16) 2 × 7

17) 7 × 9

18) 2 × 9

19) 1 × 4

20) 1 × 8

21) 2 × 6

22) 11 × 9

23) 3 × 8

24) 7 × 6

25) 6 × 5

26) 9 × 4

27) 3 × 8

28) 0 × 1

29) 0 × 5

30) 6 × 3

31) 2 × 0

32) 5 × 2

33) 0 × 2

34) 9 × 6

35) 2 × 6

Mixed Multiplication 0 To 12

1) $\begin{array}{r} 7 \\ \times\ 3 \\ \hline \end{array}$

2) $\begin{array}{r} 12 \\ \times\ 8 \\ \hline \end{array}$

3) $\begin{array}{r} 12 \\ \times\ 0 \\ \hline \end{array}$

4) $\begin{array}{r} 7 \\ \times\ 6 \\ \hline \end{array}$

5) $\begin{array}{r} 7 \\ \times\ 8 \\ \hline \end{array}$

6) $\begin{array}{r} 0 \\ \times\ 1 \\ \hline \end{array}$

7) $\begin{array}{r} 9 \\ \times\ 3 \\ \hline \end{array}$

8) $\begin{array}{r} 11 \\ \times\ 7 \\ \hline \end{array}$

9) $\begin{array}{r} 11 \\ \times\ 9 \\ \hline \end{array}$

10) $\begin{array}{r} 6 \\ \times\ 2 \\ \hline \end{array}$

11) $\begin{array}{r} 2 \\ \times\ 0 \\ \hline \end{array}$

12) $\begin{array}{r} 12 \\ \times\ 3 \\ \hline \end{array}$

13) $\begin{array}{r} 11 \\ \times\ 3 \\ \hline \end{array}$

14) $\begin{array}{r} 1 \\ \times\ 0 \\ \hline \end{array}$

15) $\begin{array}{r} 0 \\ \times\ 0 \\ \hline \end{array}$

16) $\begin{array}{r} 2 \\ \times\ 3 \\ \hline \end{array}$

17) $\begin{array}{r} 0 \\ \times\ 9 \\ \hline \end{array}$

18) $\begin{array}{r} 10 \\ \times\ 4 \\ \hline \end{array}$

19) $\begin{array}{r} 9 \\ \times\ 3 \\ \hline \end{array}$

20) $\begin{array}{r} 1 \\ \times\ 1 \\ \hline \end{array}$

21) $\begin{array}{r} 12 \\ \times\ 2 \\ \hline \end{array}$

22) $\begin{array}{r} 1 \\ \times\ 0 \\ \hline \end{array}$

23) $\begin{array}{r} 3 \\ \times\ 6 \\ \hline \end{array}$

24) $\begin{array}{r} 3 \\ \times\ 1 \\ \hline \end{array}$

25) $\begin{array}{r} 2 \\ \times\ 0 \\ \hline \end{array}$

26) $\begin{array}{r} 6 \\ \times\ 2 \\ \hline \end{array}$

27) $\begin{array}{r} 10 \\ \times\ 4 \\ \hline \end{array}$

28) $\begin{array}{r} 12 \\ \times\ 4 \\ \hline \end{array}$

29) $\begin{array}{r} 10 \\ \times\ 6 \\ \hline \end{array}$

30) $\begin{array}{r} 4 \\ \times\ 7 \\ \hline \end{array}$

31) $\begin{array}{r} 10 \\ \times\ 9 \\ \hline \end{array}$

32) $\begin{array}{r} 9 \\ \times\ 4 \\ \hline \end{array}$

33) $\begin{array}{r} 6 \\ \times\ 0 \\ \hline \end{array}$

34) $\begin{array}{r} 10 \\ \times\ 9 \\ \hline \end{array}$

35) $\begin{array}{r} 2 \\ \times\ 8 \\ \hline \end{array}$

Mixed Multiplication 0 To 12

1)
$$\begin{array}{r} 2 \\ \times\ 1 \\ \hline \end{array}$$

2)
$$\begin{array}{r} 4 \\ \times\ 2 \\ \hline \end{array}$$

3)
$$\begin{array}{r} 1 \\ \times\ 3 \\ \hline \end{array}$$

4)
$$\begin{array}{r} 6 \\ \times\ 8 \\ \hline \end{array}$$

5)
$$\begin{array}{r} 4 \\ \times\ 4 \\ \hline \end{array}$$

6)
$$\begin{array}{r} 2 \\ \times\ 1 \\ \hline \end{array}$$

7)
$$\begin{array}{r} 8 \\ \times\ 8 \\ \hline \end{array}$$

8)
$$\begin{array}{r} 7 \\ \times\ 3 \\ \hline \end{array}$$

9)
$$\begin{array}{r} 10 \\ \times\ 6 \\ \hline \end{array}$$

10)
$$\begin{array}{r} 1 \\ \times\ 9 \\ \hline \end{array}$$

11)
$$\begin{array}{r} 1 \\ \times\ 6 \\ \hline \end{array}$$

12)
$$\begin{array}{r} 7 \\ \times\ 2 \\ \hline \end{array}$$

13)
$$\begin{array}{r} 6 \\ \times\ 7 \\ \hline \end{array}$$

14)
$$\begin{array}{r} 3 \\ \times\ 6 \\ \hline \end{array}$$

15)
$$\begin{array}{r} 8 \\ \times\ 1 \\ \hline \end{array}$$

16)
$$\begin{array}{r} 12 \\ \times\ 8 \\ \hline \end{array}$$

17)
$$\begin{array}{r} 2 \\ \times\ 2 \\ \hline \end{array}$$

18)
$$\begin{array}{r} 1 \\ \times\ 6 \\ \hline \end{array}$$

19)
$$\begin{array}{r} 2 \\ \times\ 4 \\ \hline \end{array}$$

20)
$$\begin{array}{r} 4 \\ \times\ 2 \\ \hline \end{array}$$

21)
$$\begin{array}{r} 9 \\ \times\ 5 \\ \hline \end{array}$$

22)
$$\begin{array}{r} 5 \\ \times\ 0 \\ \hline \end{array}$$

23)
$$\begin{array}{r} 9 \\ \times\ 9 \\ \hline \end{array}$$

24)
$$\begin{array}{r} 8 \\ \times\ 2 \\ \hline \end{array}$$

25)
$$\begin{array}{r} 8 \\ \times\ 5 \\ \hline \end{array}$$

26)
$$\begin{array}{r} 6 \\ \times\ 0 \\ \hline \end{array}$$

27)
$$\begin{array}{r} 3 \\ \times\ 8 \\ \hline \end{array}$$

28)
$$\begin{array}{r} 5 \\ \times\ 5 \\ \hline \end{array}$$

29)
$$\begin{array}{r} 2 \\ \times\ 9 \\ \hline \end{array}$$

30)
$$\begin{array}{r} 9 \\ \times\ 4 \\ \hline \end{array}$$

31)
$$\begin{array}{r} 1 \\ \times\ 4 \\ \hline \end{array}$$

32)
$$\begin{array}{r} 11 \\ \times\ 7 \\ \hline \end{array}$$

33)
$$\begin{array}{r} 1 \\ \times\ 8 \\ \hline \end{array}$$

34)
$$\begin{array}{r} 12 \\ \times\ 9 \\ \hline \end{array}$$

35)
$$\begin{array}{r} 8 \\ \times\ 8 \\ \hline \end{array}$$

Mixed Multiplication 0 To 12

1)
$$\begin{array}{r} 8 \\ \times\ 3 \\ \hline \end{array}$$

2)
$$\begin{array}{r} 1 \\ \times\ 0 \\ \hline \end{array}$$

3)
$$\begin{array}{r} 2 \\ \times\ 8 \\ \hline \end{array}$$

4)
$$\begin{array}{r} 9 \\ \times\ 9 \\ \hline \end{array}$$

5)
$$\begin{array}{r} 12 \\ \times\ 0 \\ \hline \end{array}$$

6)
$$\begin{array}{r} 3 \\ \times\ 0 \\ \hline \end{array}$$

7)
$$\begin{array}{r} 7 \\ \times\ 3 \\ \hline \end{array}$$

8)
$$\begin{array}{r} 2 \\ \times\ 4 \\ \hline \end{array}$$

9)
$$\begin{array}{r} 9 \\ \times\ 1 \\ \hline \end{array}$$

10)
$$\begin{array}{r} 5 \\ \times\ 8 \\ \hline \end{array}$$

11)
$$\begin{array}{r} 5 \\ \times\ 7 \\ \hline \end{array}$$

12)
$$\begin{array}{r} 5 \\ \times\ 7 \\ \hline \end{array}$$

13)
$$\begin{array}{r} 4 \\ \times\ 0 \\ \hline \end{array}$$

14)
$$\begin{array}{r} 10 \\ \times\ 3 \\ \hline \end{array}$$

15)
$$\begin{array}{r} 1 \\ \times\ 0 \\ \hline \end{array}$$

16)
$$\begin{array}{r} 9 \\ \times\ 9 \\ \hline \end{array}$$

17)
$$\begin{array}{r} 12 \\ \times\ 1 \\ \hline \end{array}$$

18)
$$\begin{array}{r} 7 \\ \times\ 6 \\ \hline \end{array}$$

19)
$$\begin{array}{r} 10 \\ \times\ 2 \\ \hline \end{array}$$

20)
$$\begin{array}{r} 7 \\ \times\ 7 \\ \hline \end{array}$$

21)
$$\begin{array}{r} 10 \\ \times\ 1 \\ \hline \end{array}$$

22)
$$\begin{array}{r} 4 \\ \times\ 2 \\ \hline \end{array}$$

23)
$$\begin{array}{r} 1 \\ \times\ 8 \\ \hline \end{array}$$

24)
$$\begin{array}{r} 9 \\ \times\ 9 \\ \hline \end{array}$$

25)
$$\begin{array}{r} 9 \\ \times\ 4 \\ \hline \end{array}$$

26)
$$\begin{array}{r} 3 \\ \times\ 6 \\ \hline \end{array}$$

27)
$$\begin{array}{r} 11 \\ \times\ 1 \\ \hline \end{array}$$

28)
$$\begin{array}{r} 12 \\ \times\ 3 \\ \hline \end{array}$$

29)
$$\begin{array}{r} 0 \\ \times\ 3 \\ \hline \end{array}$$

30)
$$\begin{array}{r} 11 \\ \times\ 5 \\ \hline \end{array}$$

31)
$$\begin{array}{r} 7 \\ \times\ 8 \\ \hline \end{array}$$

32)
$$\begin{array}{r} 3 \\ \times\ 9 \\ \hline \end{array}$$

33)
$$\begin{array}{r} 8 \\ \times\ 5 \\ \hline \end{array}$$

34)
$$\begin{array}{r} 9 \\ \times\ 8 \\ \hline \end{array}$$

35)
$$\begin{array}{r} 9 \\ \times\ 1 \\ \hline \end{array}$$

PART 2:

DIVISION PRACTICE

Division Timed Tests
(Tables 0 To 12)

Let's Divide By 0 & 1

1) $\begin{array}{r} 2 \\ \div\ 1 \\ \hline \end{array}$

2) $\begin{array}{r} 3 \\ \div\ 0 \\ \hline \end{array}$

3) $\begin{array}{r} 2 \\ \div\ 1 \\ \hline \end{array}$

4) $\begin{array}{r} 7 \\ \div\ 1 \\ \hline \end{array}$

5) $\begin{array}{r} 5 \\ \div\ 1 \\ \hline \end{array}$

6) $\begin{array}{r} 10 \\ \div\ 0 \\ \hline \end{array}$

7) $\begin{array}{r} 6 \\ \div\ 1 \\ \hline \end{array}$

8) $\begin{array}{r} 3 \\ \div\ 1 \\ \hline \end{array}$

9) $\begin{array}{r} 7 \\ \div\ 1 \\ \hline \end{array}$

10) $\begin{array}{r} 10 \\ \div\ 1 \\ \hline \end{array}$

11) $\begin{array}{r} 2 \\ \div\ 1 \\ \hline \end{array}$

12) $\begin{array}{r} 7 \\ \div\ 1 \\ \hline \end{array}$

13) $\begin{array}{r} 6 \\ \div\ 1 \\ \hline \end{array}$

14) $\begin{array}{r} 6 \\ \div\ 1 \\ \hline \end{array}$

15) $\begin{array}{r} 1 \\ \div\ 1 \\ \hline \end{array}$

16) $\begin{array}{r} 6 \\ \div\ 1 \\ \hline \end{array}$

17) $\begin{array}{r} 2 \\ \div\ 0 \\ \hline \end{array}$

18) $\begin{array}{r} 6 \\ \div\ 1 \\ \hline \end{array}$

19) $\begin{array}{r} 4 \\ \div\ 1 \\ \hline \end{array}$

20) $\begin{array}{r} 9 \\ \div\ 1 \\ \hline \end{array}$

21) $\begin{array}{r} 9 \\ \div\ 1 \\ \hline \end{array}$

22) $\begin{array}{r} 4 \\ \div\ 1 \\ \hline \end{array}$

23) $\begin{array}{r} 7 \\ \div\ 1 \\ \hline \end{array}$

24) $\begin{array}{r} 8 \\ \div\ 1 \\ \hline \end{array}$

25) $\begin{array}{r} 6 \\ \div\ 1 \\ \hline \end{array}$

26) $\begin{array}{r} 8 \\ \div\ 1 \\ \hline \end{array}$

27) $\begin{array}{r} 10 \\ \div\ 1 \\ \hline \end{array}$

28) $\begin{array}{r} 3 \\ \div\ 1 \\ \hline \end{array}$

29) $\begin{array}{r} 10 \\ \div\ 1 \\ \hline \end{array}$

30) $\begin{array}{r} 1 \\ \div\ 1 \\ \hline \end{array}$

31) $\begin{array}{r} 8 \\ \div\ 1 \\ \hline \end{array}$

32) $\begin{array}{r} 5 \\ \div\ 1 \\ \hline \end{array}$

33) $\begin{array}{r} 4 \\ \div\ 1 \\ \hline \end{array}$

34) $\begin{array}{r} 9 \\ \div\ 1 \\ \hline \end{array}$

35) $\begin{array}{r} 4 \\ \div\ 1 \\ \hline \end{array}$

Let's Divide By 0 & 1

1) $9 \div 1$

2) $1 \div 1$

3) $4 \div 1$

4) $1 \div 1$

5) $7 \div 1$

6) $1 \div 1$

7) $1 \div 1$

8) $5 \div 1$

9) $9 \div 1$

10) $3 \div 1$

11) $3 \div 1$

12) $1 \div 1$

13) $6 \div 1$

14) $7 \div 1$

15) $10 \div 1$

16) $8 \div 1$

17) $2 \div 1$

18) $2 \div 1$

19) $8 \div 0$

20) $8 \div 1$

21) $5 \div 1$

22) $8 \div 1$

23) $4 \div 0$

24) $6 \div 1$

25) $1 \div 1$

26) $3 \div 1$

27) $10 \div 0$

28) $6 \div 1$

29) $4 \div 1$

30) $5 \div 1$

31) $7 \div 1$

32) $3 \div 1$

33) $4 \div 1$

34) $1 \div 1$

35) $10 \div 1$

Let's Divide By 0 & 1

1) $10 \div 1$

2) $10 \div 1$

3) $7 \div 1$

4) $7 \div 1$

5) $2 \div 1$

6) $1 \div 1$

7) $8 \div 1$

8) $3 \div 1$

9) $10 \div 1$

10) $1 \div 1$

11) $2 \div 1$

12) $7 \div 1$

13) $3 \div 1$

14) $10 \div 1$

15) $1 \div 1$

16) $4 \div 1$

17) $4 \div 1$

18) $8 \div 1$

19) $1 \div 1$

20) $3 \div 1$

21) $5 \div 1$

22) $2 \div 0$

23) $9 \div 1$

24) $6 \div 0$

25) $4 \div 1$

26) $1 \div 1$

27) $1 \div 1$

28) $9 \div 1$

29) $10 \div 1$

30) $3 \div 1$

31) $7 \div 1$

32) $9 \div 1$

33) $6 \div 1$

34) $3 \div 1$

35) $1 \div 0$

Let's Divide By 0 & 1

1) 5 ÷ 1

2) 8 ÷ 1

3) 5 ÷ 1

4) 7 ÷ 1

5) 7 ÷ 1

6) 9 ÷ 1

7) 3 ÷ 1

8) 1 ÷ 1

9) 5 ÷ 0

10) 3 ÷ 0

11) 4 ÷ 1

12) 6 ÷ 1

13) 4 ÷ 1

14) 7 ÷ 1

15) 2 ÷ 1

16) 7 ÷ 1

17) 8 ÷ 1

18) 8 ÷ 1

19) 8 ÷ 1

20) 2 ÷ 1

21) 4 ÷ 1

22) 6 ÷ 1

23) 3 ÷ 0

24) 3 ÷ 1

25) 5 ÷ 1

26) 4 ÷ 1

27) 6 ÷ 1

28) 2 ÷ 1

29) 10 ÷ 1

30) 6 ÷ 1

31) 5 ÷ 1

32) 6 ÷ 1

33) 2 ÷ 1

34) 3 ÷ 1

35) 10 ÷ 1

Let's Divide By 2

1) $4 \div 2$

2) $12 \div 2$

3) $16 \div 2$

4) $14 \div 2$

5) $12 \div 2$

6) $14 \div 2$

7) $20 \div 2$

8) $10 \div 2$

9) $20 \div 2$

10) $16 \div 2$

11) $20 \div 2$

12) $12 \div 2$

13) $16 \div 2$

14) $18 \div 2$

15) $20 \div 2$

16) $4 \div 2$

17) $6 \div 2$

18) $2 \div 2$

19) $12 \div 2$

20) $20 \div 2$

21) $6 \div 2$

22) $6 \div 2$

23) $4 \div 2$

24) $4 \div 2$

25) $18 \div 2$

26) $8 \div 2$

27) $16 \div 2$

28) $6 \div 2$

29) $12 \div 2$

30) $12 \div 2$

31) $10 \div 2$

32) $8 \div 2$

33) $16 \div 2$

34) $6 \div 2$

35) $12 \div 2$

Date: Name: Score:

Let's Divide By 2

1) $16 \div 2$

2) $4 \div 2$

3) $2 \div 2$

4) $18 \div 2$

5) $12 \div 2$

6) $14 \div 2$

7) $14 \div 2$

8) $18 \div 2$

9) $20 \div 2$

10) $4 \div 2$

11) $20 \div 2$

12) $6 \div 2$

13) $18 \div 2$

14) $18 \div 2$

15) $16 \div 2$

16) $14 \div 2$

17) $18 \div 2$

18) $18 \div 2$

19) $16 \div 2$

20) $6 \div 2$

21) $8 \div 2$

22) $18 \div 2$

23) $12 \div 2$

24) $6 \div 2$

25) $14 \div 2$

26) $6 \div 2$

27) $6 \div 2$

28) $14 \div 2$

29) $16 \div 2$

30) $2 \div 2$

31) $16 \div 2$

32) $2 \div 2$

33) $14 \div 2$

34) $6 \div 2$

35) $8 \div 2$

Let's Divide By 2

1) $18 \div 2$

2) $4 \div 2$

3) $8 \div 2$

4) $16 \div 2$

5) $2 \div 2$

6) $4 \div 2$

7) $14 \div 2$

8) $8 \div 2$

9) $10 \div 2$

10) $20 \div 2$

11) $6 \div 2$

12) $14 \div 2$

13) $8 \div 2$

14) $8 \div 2$

15) $18 \div 2$

16) $20 \div 2$

17) $20 \div 2$

18) $14 \div 2$

19) $12 \div 2$

20) $4 \div 2$

21) $10 \div 2$

22) $4 \div 2$

23) $18 \div 2$

24) $14 \div 2$

25) $18 \div 2$

26) $12 \div 2$

27) $2 \div 2$

28) $8 \div 2$

29) $2 \div 2$

30) $18 \div 2$

31) $4 \div 2$

32) $10 \div 2$

33) $10 \div 2$

34) $20 \div 2$

35) $10 \div 2$

Let's Divide By 2

1) 4 ÷ 2

2) 8 ÷ 2

3) 16 ÷ 2

4) 14 ÷ 2

5) 16 ÷ 2

6) 20 ÷ 2

7) 16 ÷ 2

8) 10 ÷ 2

9) 4 ÷ 2

10) 14 ÷ 2

11) 6 ÷ 2

12) 16 ÷ 2

13) 20 ÷ 2

14) 4 ÷ 2

15) 16 ÷ 2

16) 4 ÷ 2

17) 12 ÷ 2

18) 10 ÷ 2

19) 20 ÷ 2

20) 4 ÷ 2

21) 2 ÷ 2

22) 8 ÷ 2

23) 8 ÷ 2

24) 8 ÷ 2

25) 6 ÷ 2

26) 18 ÷ 2

27) 14 ÷ 2

28) 8 ÷ 2

29) 6 ÷ 2

30) 4 ÷ 2

31) 8 ÷ 2

32) 6 ÷ 2

33) 18 ÷ 2

34) 10 ÷ 2

35) 16 ÷ 2

Let's Divide By 3

1) $24 \div 3$

2) $24 \div 3$

3) $3 \div 3$

4) $12 \div 3$

5) $6 \div 3$

6) $18 \div 3$

7) $18 \div 3$

8) $21 \div 3$

9) $21 \div 3$

10) $21 \div 3$

11) $21 \div 3$

12) $12 \div 3$

13) $3 \div 3$

14) $18 \div 3$

15) $21 \div 3$

16) $12 \div 3$

17) $24 \div 3$

18) $30 \div 3$

19) $9 \div 3$

20) $24 \div 3$

21) $27 \div 3$

22) $9 \div 3$

23) $15 \div 3$

24) $21 \div 3$

25) $30 \div 3$

26) $21 \div 3$

27) $9 \div 3$

28) $9 \div 3$

29) $30 \div 3$

30) $21 \div 3$

31) $21 \div 3$

32) $18 \div 3$

33) $3 \div 3$

34) $9 \div 3$

35) $9 \div 3$

Let's Divide By 3

1) 24 ÷ 3

2) 9 ÷ 3

3) 27 ÷ 3

4) 15 ÷ 3

5) 30 ÷ 3

6) 21 ÷ 3

7) 24 ÷ 3

8) 9 ÷ 3

9) 6 ÷ 3

10) 6 ÷ 3

11) 30 ÷ 3

12) 9 ÷ 3

13) 6 ÷ 3

14) 30 ÷ 3

15) 27 ÷ 3

16) 18 ÷ 3

17) 18 ÷ 3

18) 24 ÷ 3

19) 18 ÷ 3

20) 3 ÷ 3

21) 12 ÷ 3

22) 12 ÷ 3

23) 12 ÷ 3

24) 12 ÷ 3

25) 9 ÷ 3

26) 18 ÷ 3

27) 6 ÷ 3

28) 30 ÷ 3

29) 9 ÷ 3

30) 3 ÷ 3

31) 24 ÷ 3

32) 27 ÷ 3

33) 24 ÷ 3

34) 15 ÷ 3

35) 9 ÷ 3

Let's Divide By 3

1) $6 \div 3$

2) $24 \div 3$

3) $21 \div 3$

4) $6 \div 3$

5) $18 \div 3$

6) $9 \div 3$

7) $6 \div 3$

8) $12 \div 3$

9) $12 \div 3$

10) $30 \div 3$

11) $27 \div 3$

12) $12 \div 3$

13) $12 \div 3$

14) $9 \div 3$

15) $15 \div 3$

16) $18 \div 3$

17) $30 \div 3$

18) $21 \div 3$

19) $12 \div 3$

20) $15 \div 3$

21) $27 \div 3$

22) $9 \div 3$

23) $9 \div 3$

24) $24 \div 3$

25) $30 \div 3$

26) $12 \div 3$

27) $12 \div 3$

28) $21 \div 3$

29) $6 \div 3$

30) $30 \div 3$

31) $30 \div 3$

32) $24 \div 3$

33) $12 \div 3$

34) $27 \div 3$

35) $30 \div 3$

Let's Divide By 3

1) 24 ÷ 3

2) 21 ÷ 3

3) 3 ÷ 3

4) 3 ÷ 3

5) 24 ÷ 3

6) 18 ÷ 3

7) 18 ÷ 3

8) 3 ÷ 3

9) 15 ÷ 3

10) 24 ÷ 3

11) 6 ÷ 3

12) 30 ÷ 3

13) 9 ÷ 3

14) 18 ÷ 3

15) 21 ÷ 3

16) 18 ÷ 3

17) 15 ÷ 3

18) 18 ÷ 3

19) 27 ÷ 3

20) 6 ÷ 3

21) 6 ÷ 3

22) 21 ÷ 3

23) 21 ÷ 3

24) 24 ÷ 3

25) 12 ÷ 3

26) 9 ÷ 3

27) 30 ÷ 3

28) 12 ÷ 3

29) 21 ÷ 3

30) 12 ÷ 3

31) 3 ÷ 3

32) 3 ÷ 3

33) 24 ÷ 3

34) 21 ÷ 3

35) 18 ÷ 3

Let's Divide By 4

1) $32 \div 4$

2) $36 \div 4$

3) $32 \div 4$

4) $16 \div 4$

5) $20 \div 4$

6) $32 \div 4$

7) $16 \div 4$

8) $40 \div 4$

9) $4 \div 4$

10) $24 \div 4$

11) $20 \div 4$

12) $28 \div 4$

13) $12 \div 4$

14) $40 \div 4$

15) $4 \div 4$

16) $36 \div 4$

17) $16 \div 4$

18) $12 \div 4$

19) $20 \div 4$

20) $24 \div 4$

21) $12 \div 4$

22) $12 \div 4$

23) $32 \div 4$

24) $12 \div 4$

25) $36 \div 4$

26) $20 \div 4$

27) $8 \div 4$

28) $32 \div 4$

29) $40 \div 4$

30) $28 \div 4$

31) $28 \div 4$

32) $32 \div 4$

33) $20 \div 4$

34) $24 \div 4$

35) $16 \div 4$

Let's Divide By 4

1) $40 \div 4$

2) $40 \div 4$

3) $12 \div 4$

4) $24 \div 4$

5) $16 \div 4$

6) $16 \div 4$

7) $8 \div 4$

8) $12 \div 4$

9) $40 \div 4$

10) $16 \div 4$

11) $4 \div 4$

12) $16 \div 4$

13) $16 \div 4$

14) $16 \div 4$

15) $28 \div 4$

16) $24 \div 4$

17) $20 \div 4$

18) $36 \div 4$

19) $40 \div 4$

20) $36 \div 4$

21) $24 \div 4$

22) $12 \div 4$

23) $4 \div 4$

24) $28 \div 4$

25) $24 \div 4$

26) $4 \div 4$

27) $40 \div 4$

28) $36 \div 4$

29) $20 \div 4$

30) $28 \div 4$

31) $40 \div 4$

32) $32 \div 4$

33) $4 \div 4$

34) $12 \div 4$

35) $32 \div 4$

Let's Divide By 4

1)   12 ÷ 4

2)   28 ÷ 4

3)   40 ÷ 4

4)   20 ÷ 4

5)   40 ÷ 4

6)   16 ÷ 4

7)   24 ÷ 4

8)   32 ÷ 4

9)   24 ÷ 4

10)   4 ÷ 4

11)   8 ÷ 4

12)   24 ÷ 4

13)   12 ÷ 4

14)   36 ÷ 4

15)   24 ÷ 4

16)   36 ÷ 4

17)   28 ÷ 4

18)   8 ÷ 4

19)   32 ÷ 4

20)   28 ÷ 4

21)   28 ÷ 4

22)   4 ÷ 4

23)   12 ÷ 4

24)   24 ÷ 4

25)   36 ÷ 4

26)   4 ÷ 4

27)   28 ÷ 4

28)   12 ÷ 4

29)   28 ÷ 4

30)   16 ÷ 4

31)   32 ÷ 4

32)   16 ÷ 4

33)   24 ÷ 4

34)   20 ÷ 4

35)   8 ÷ 4

Let's Divide By 4

1) $24 \div 4 =$

2) $4 \div 4 =$

3) $12 \div 4 =$

4) $16 \div 4 =$

5) $28 \div 4 =$

6) $12 \div 4 =$

7) $12 \div 4 =$

8) $32 \div 4 =$

9) $4 \div 4 =$

10) $24 \div 4 =$

11) $40 \div 4 =$

12) $8 \div 4 =$

13) $28 \div 4 =$

14) $12 \div 4 =$

15) $8 \div 4 =$

16) $32 \div 4 =$

17) $16 \div 4 =$

18) $32 \div 4 =$

19) $28 \div 4 =$

20) $4 \div 4 =$

21) $16 \div 4 =$

22) $40 \div 4 =$

23) $20 \div 4 =$

24) $36 \div 4 =$

25) $28 \div 4 =$

26) $32 \div 4 =$

27) $20 \div 4 =$

28) $16 \div 4 =$

29) $4 \div 4 =$

30) $36 \div 4 =$

31) $28 \div 4 =$

32) $36 \div 4 =$

33) $28 \div 4 =$

34) $28 \div 4 =$

35) $32 \div 4 =$

Let's Divide By 5

1) $10 \div 5$

2) $5 \div 5$

3) $40 \div 5$

4) $10 \div 5$

5) $25 \div 5$

6) $50 \div 5$

7) $25 \div 5$

8) $50 \div 5$

9) $25 \div 5$

10) $20 \div 5$

11) $45 \div 5$

12) $30 \div 5$

13) $40 \div 5$

14) $30 \div 5$

15) $50 \div 5$

16) $35 \div 5$

17) $20 \div 5$

18) $15 \div 5$

19) $5 \div 5$

20) $15 \div 5$

21) $15 \div 5$

22) $25 \div 5$

23) $35 \div 5$

24) $15 \div 5$

25) $5 \div 5$

26) $25 \div 5$

27) $30 \div 5$

28) $45 \div 5$

29) $10 \div 5$

30) $25 \div 5$

31) $40 \div 5$

32) $30 \div 5$

33) $35 \div 5$

34) $15 \div 5$

35) $25 \div 5$

Let's Divide By 5

1) $35 \div 5$

2) $50 \div 5$

3) $5 \div 5$

4) $40 \div 5$

5) $20 \div 5$

6) $5 \div 5$

7) $20 \div 5$

8) $5 \div 5$

9) $5 \div 5$

10) $15 \div 5$

11) $5 \div 5$

12) $35 \div 5$

13) $25 \div 5$

14) $10 \div 5$

15) $20 \div 5$

16) $5 \div 5$

17) $5 \div 5$

18) $15 \div 5$

19) $40 \div 5$

20) $5 \div 5$

21) $5 \div 5$

22) $45 \div 5$

23) $15 \div 5$

24) $25 \div 5$

25) $15 \div 5$

26) $15 \div 5$

27) $40 \div 5$

28) $45 \div 5$

29) $40 \div 5$

30) $50 \div 5$

31) $35 \div 5$

32) $15 \div 5$

33) $50 \div 5$

34) $10 \div 5$

35) $40 \div 5$

Let's Divide By 5

1) $45 \div 5$

2) $20 \div 5$

3) $30 \div 5$

4) $50 \div 5$

5) $30 \div 5$

6) $5 \div 5$

7) $45 \div 5$

8) $15 \div 5$

9) $20 \div 5$

10) $50 \div 5$

11) $5 \div 5$

12) $20 \div 5$

13) $50 \div 5$

14) $20 \div 5$

15) $45 \div 5$

16) $15 \div 5$

17) $15 \div 5$

18) $30 \div 5$

19) $45 \div 5$

20) $20 \div 5$

21) $45 \div 5$

22) $10 \div 5$

23) $15 \div 5$

24) $15 \div 5$

25) $45 \div 5$

26) $45 \div 5$

27) $25 \div 5$

28) $35 \div 5$

29) $30 \div 5$

30) $10 \div 5$

31) $45 \div 5$

32) $25 \div 5$

33) $10 \div 5$

34) $10 \div 5$

35) $15 \div 5$

Let's Divide By 5

1) 40 ÷ 5

2) 25 ÷ 5

3) 45 ÷ 5

4) 45 ÷ 5

5) 20 ÷ 5

6) 5 ÷ 5

7) 35 ÷ 5

8) 50 ÷ 5

9) 5 ÷ 5

10) 45 ÷ 5

11) 35 ÷ 5

12) 45 ÷ 5

13) 40 ÷ 5

14) 50 ÷ 5

15) 5 ÷ 5

16) 50 ÷ 5

17) 35 ÷ 5

18) 5 ÷ 5

19) 35 ÷ 5

20) 50 ÷ 5

21) 20 ÷ 5

22) 45 ÷ 5

23) 15 ÷ 5

24) 15 ÷ 5

25) 15 ÷ 5

26) 40 ÷ 5

27) 35 ÷ 5

28) 15 ÷ 5

29) 20 ÷ 5

30) 50 ÷ 5

31) 25 ÷ 5

32) 45 ÷ 5

33) 45 ÷ 5

34) 10 ÷ 5

35) 30 ÷ 5

Let's Divide By 6

1) $54 \div 6$

2) $18 \div 6$

3) $30 \div 6$

4) $48 \div 6$

5) $42 \div 6$

6) $36 \div 6$

7) $48 \div 6$

8) $12 \div 6$

9) $12 \div 6$

10) $30 \div 6$

11) $48 \div 6$

12) $48 \div 6$

13) $60 \div 6$

14) $60 \div 6$

15) $12 \div 6$

16) $42 \div 6$

17) $48 \div 6$

18) $36 \div 6$

19) $60 \div 6$

20) $12 \div 6$

21) $24 \div 6$

22) $60 \div 6$

23) $30 \div 6$

24) $18 \div 6$

25) $12 \div 6$

26) $54 \div 6$

27) $48 \div 6$

28) $24 \div 6$

29) $36 \div 6$

30) $6 \div 6$

31) $60 \div 6$

32) $6 \div 6$

33) $18 \div 6$

34) $18 \div 6$

35) $24 \div 6$

Let's Divide By 6

1) 60 ÷ 6

2) 54 ÷ 6

3) 6 ÷ 6

4) 42 ÷ 6

5) 18 ÷ 6

6) 42 ÷ 6

7) 6 ÷ 6

8) 36 ÷ 6

9) 42 ÷ 6

10) 48 ÷ 6

11) 48 ÷ 6

12) 36 ÷ 6

13) 12 ÷ 6

14) 48 ÷ 6

15) 42 ÷ 6

16) 60 ÷ 6

17) 54 ÷ 6

18) 48 ÷ 6

19) 54 ÷ 6

20) 12 ÷ 6

21) 60 ÷ 6

22) 30 ÷ 6

23) 60 ÷ 6

24) 48 ÷ 6

25) 54 ÷ 6

26) 60 ÷ 6

27) 48 ÷ 6

28) 60 ÷ 6

29) 60 ÷ 6

30) 30 ÷ 6

31) 54 ÷ 6

32) 30 ÷ 6

33) 24 ÷ 6

34) 6 ÷ 6

35) 36 ÷ 6

Let's Divide By 6

1) $60 \div 6$

2) $48 \div 6$

3) $18 \div 6$

4) $60 \div 6$

5) $30 \div 6$

6) $12 \div 6$

7) $42 \div 6$

8) $54 \div 6$

9) $24 \div 6$

10) $24 \div 6$

11) $42 \div 6$

12) $48 \div 6$

13) $42 \div 6$

14) $36 \div 6$

15) $30 \div 6$

16) $48 \div 6$

17) $42 \div 6$

18) $42 \div 6$

19) $18 \div 6$

20) $48 \div 6$

21) $6 \div 6$

22) $42 \div 6$

23) $12 \div 6$

24) $60 \div 6$

25) $36 \div 6$

26) $42 \div 6$

27) $6 \div 6$

28) $60 \div 6$

29) $60 \div 6$

30) $12 \div 6$

31) $24 \div 6$

32) $54 \div 6$

33) $54 \div 6$

34) $42 \div 6$

35) $36 \div 6$

Let's Divide By 6

1)
$$6 \div 6$$

2)
$$36 \div 6$$

3)
$$42 \div 6$$

4)
$$12 \div 6$$

5)
$$60 \div 6$$

6)
$$42 \div 6$$

7)
$$36 \div 6$$

8)
$$60 \div 6$$

9)
$$18 \div 6$$

10)
$$36 \div 6$$

11)
$$30 \div 6$$

12)
$$24 \div 6$$

13)
$$48 \div 6$$

14)
$$36 \div 6$$

15)
$$12 \div 6$$

16)
$$24 \div 6$$

17)
$$30 \div 6$$

18)
$$48 \div 6$$

19)
$$60 \div 6$$

20)
$$6 \div 6$$

21)
$$42 \div 6$$

22)
$$18 \div 6$$

23)
$$6 \div 6$$

24)
$$6 \div 6$$

25)
$$24 \div 6$$

26)
$$60 \div 6$$

27)
$$24 \div 6$$

28)
$$30 \div 6$$

29)
$$24 \div 6$$

30)
$$6 \div 6$$

31)
$$48 \div 6$$

32)
$$12 \div 6$$

33)
$$54 \div 6$$

34)
$$18 \div 6$$

35)
$$48 \div 6$$

Let's Divide By 7

1) $70 \div 7$

2) $49 \div 7$

3) $28 \div 7$

4) $56 \div 7$

5) $56 \div 7$

6) $28 \div 7$

7) $42 \div 7$

8) $21 \div 7$

9) $63 \div 7$

10) $28 \div 7$

11) $42 \div 7$

12) $63 \div 7$

13) $56 \div 7$

14) $70 \div 7$

15) $14 \div 7$

16) $42 \div 7$

17) $56 \div 7$

18) $7 \div 7$

19) $56 \div 7$

20) $35 \div 7$

21) $14 \div 7$

22) $7 \div 7$

23) $28 \div 7$

24) $14 \div 7$

25) $35 \div 7$

26) $14 \div 7$

27) $63 \div 7$

28) $42 \div 7$

29) $42 \div 7$

30) $21 \div 7$

31) $28 \div 7$

32) $14 \div 7$

33) $56 \div 7$

34) $49 \div 7$

35) $7 \div 7$

Let's Divide By 7

1) $14 \div 7$

2) $56 \div 7$

3) $28 \div 7$

4) $7 \div 7$

5) $70 \div 7$

6) $56 \div 7$

7) $56 \div 7$

8) $21 \div 7$

9) $14 \div 7$

10) $28 \div 7$

11) $56 \div 7$

12) $21 \div 7$

13) $35 \div 7$

14) $21 \div 7$

15) $21 \div 7$

16) $63 \div 7$

17) $56 \div 7$

18) $7 \div 7$

19) $63 \div 7$

20) $63 \div 7$

21) $70 \div 7$

22) $70 \div 7$

23) $56 \div 7$

24) $49 \div 7$

25) $42 \div 7$

26) $70 \div 7$

27) $42 \div 7$

28) $28 \div 7$

29) $7 \div 7$

30) $56 \div 7$

31) $56 \div 7$

32) $7 \div 7$

33) $14 \div 7$

34) $14 \div 7$

35) $63 \div 7$

Let's Divide By 7

1) $7 \div 7$

2) $14 \div 7$

3) $14 \div 7$

4) $56 \div 7$

5) $7 \div 7$

6) $70 \div 7$

7) $42 \div 7$

8) $63 \div 7$

9) $56 \div 7$

10) $56 \div 7$

11) $7 \div 7$

12) $21 \div 7$

13) $35 \div 7$

14) $49 \div 7$

15) $7 \div 7$

16) $35 \div 7$

17) $7 \div 7$

18) $28 \div 7$

19) $14 \div 7$

20) $42 \div 7$

21) $28 \div 7$

22) $70 \div 7$

23) $42 \div 7$

24) $49 \div 7$

25) $28 \div 7$

26) $56 \div 7$

27) $49 \div 7$

28) $28 \div 7$

29) $70 \div 7$

30) $21 \div 7$

31) $21 \div 7$

32) $21 \div 7$

33) $21 \div 7$

34) $49 \div 7$

35) $49 \div 7$

Let's Divide By 7

1)
$$21 \div 7$$

2)
$$42 \div 7$$

3)
$$28 \div 7$$

4)
$$28 \div 7$$

5)
$$70 \div 7$$

6)
$$14 \div 7$$

7)
$$35 \div 7$$

8)
$$7 \div 7$$

9)
$$63 \div 7$$

10)
$$42 \div 7$$

11)
$$21 \div 7$$

12)
$$35 \div 7$$

13)
$$63 \div 7$$

14)
$$28 \div 7$$

15)
$$21 \div 7$$

16)
$$70 \div 7$$

17)
$$49 \div 7$$

18)
$$63 \div 7$$

19)
$$70 \div 7$$

20)
$$7 \div 7$$

21)
$$49 \div 7$$

22)
$$56 \div 7$$

23)
$$21 \div 7$$

24)
$$42 \div 7$$

25)
$$21 \div 7$$

26)
$$49 \div 7$$

27)
$$70 \div 7$$

28)
$$7 \div 7$$

29)
$$56 \div 7$$

30)
$$7 \div 7$$

31)
$$14 \div 7$$

32)
$$49 \div 7$$

33)
$$49 \div 7$$

34)
$$56 \div 7$$

35)
$$49 \div 7$$

Let's Divide By 8

1) $40 \div 8$

2) $8 \div 8$

3) $72 \div 8$

4) $48 \div 8$

5) $32 \div 8$

6) $24 \div 8$

7) $8 \div 8$

8) $32 \div 8$

9) $64 \div 8$

10) $40 \div 8$

11) $8 \div 8$

12) $48 \div 8$

13) $8 \div 8$

14) $56 \div 8$

15) $48 \div 8$

16) $56 \div 8$

17) $32 \div 8$

18) $16 \div 8$

19) $40 \div 8$

20) $24 \div 8$

21) $80 \div 8$

22) $24 \div 8$

23) $40 \div 8$

24) $72 \div 8$

25) $48 \div 8$

26) $32 \div 8$

27) $16 \div 8$

28) $24 \div 8$

29) $64 \div 8$

30) $32 \div 8$

31) $72 \div 8$

32) $8 \div 8$

33) $8 \div 8$

34) $48 \div 8$

35) $24 \div 8$

Let's Divide By 8

1)   64 ÷ 8

2)   48 ÷ 8

3)   72 ÷ 8

4)   24 ÷ 8

5)   72 ÷ 8

6)   56 ÷ 8

7)   56 ÷ 8

8)   56 ÷ 8

9)   72 ÷ 8

10)   24 ÷ 8

11)   48 ÷ 8

12)   56 ÷ 8

13)   56 ÷ 8

14)   40 ÷ 8

15)   8 ÷ 8

16)   8 ÷ 8

17)   8 ÷ 8

18)   32 ÷ 8

19)   56 ÷ 8

20)   16 ÷ 8

21)   80 ÷ 8

22)   8 ÷ 8

23)   24 ÷ 8

24)   32 ÷ 8

25)   72 ÷ 8

26)   8 ÷ 8

27)   48 ÷ 8

28)   40 ÷ 8

29)   32 ÷ 8

30)   40 ÷ 8

31)   80 ÷ 8

32)   16 ÷ 8

33)   40 ÷ 8

34)   32 ÷ 8

35)   24 ÷ 8

Let's Divide By 8

1) 72 ÷ 8

2) 32 ÷ 8

3) 8 ÷ 8

4) 40 ÷ 8

5) 72 ÷ 8

6) 48 ÷ 8

7) 48 ÷ 8

8) 64 ÷ 8

9) 72 ÷ 8

10) 72 ÷ 8

11) 80 ÷ 8

12) 40 ÷ 8

13) 80 ÷ 8

14) 72 ÷ 8

15) 80 ÷ 8

16) 72 ÷ 8

17) 56 ÷ 8

18) 64 ÷ 8

19) 32 ÷ 8

20) 48 ÷ 8

21) 40 ÷ 8

22) 32 ÷ 8

23) 64 ÷ 8

24) 24 ÷ 8

25) 80 ÷ 8

26) 8 ÷ 8

27) 40 ÷ 8

28) 8 ÷ 8

29) 56 ÷ 8

30) 40 ÷ 8

31) 16 ÷ 8

32) 48 ÷ 8

33) 40 ÷ 8

34) 24 ÷ 8

35) 8 ÷ 8

Let's Divide By 8

1) $48 \div 8$

2) $8 \div 8$

3) $72 \div 8$

4) $8 \div 8$

5) $64 \div 8$

6) $80 \div 8$

7) $32 \div 8$

8) $48 \div 8$

9) $80 \div 8$

10) $48 \div 8$

11) $16 \div 8$

12) $24 \div 8$

13) $80 \div 8$

14) $80 \div 8$

15) $48 \div 8$

16) $56 \div 8$

17) $8 \div 8$

18) $40 \div 8$

19) $64 \div 8$

20) $32 \div 8$

21) $16 \div 8$

22) $64 \div 8$

23) $48 \div 8$

24) $48 \div 8$

25) $16 \div 8$

26) $40 \div 8$

27) $8 \div 8$

28) $56 \div 8$

29) $40 \div 8$

30) $72 \div 8$

31) $64 \div 8$

32) $72 \div 8$

33) $80 \div 8$

34) $8 \div 8$

35) $64 \div 8$

Let's Divide By 9

1) 54 ÷ 9

2) 27 ÷ 9

3) 72 ÷ 9

4) 63 ÷ 9

5) 27 ÷ 9

6) 45 ÷ 9

7) 81 ÷ 9

8) 9 ÷ 9

9) 36 ÷ 9

10) 36 ÷ 9

11) 36 ÷ 9

12) 54 ÷ 9

13) 90 ÷ 9

14) 18 ÷ 9

15) 36 ÷ 9

16) 18 ÷ 9

17) 72 ÷ 9

18) 36 ÷ 9

19) 81 ÷ 9

20) 54 ÷ 9

21) 9 ÷ 9

22) 27 ÷ 9

23) 72 ÷ 9

24) 27 ÷ 9

25) 18 ÷ 9

26) 36 ÷ 9

27) 36 ÷ 9

28) 72 ÷ 9

29) 54 ÷ 9

30) 36 ÷ 9

31) 36 ÷ 9

32) 72 ÷ 9

33) 45 ÷ 9

34) 9 ÷ 9

35) 36 ÷ 9

Let's Divide By 9

1) $72 \div 9$

2) $63 \div 9$

3) $63 \div 9$

4) $18 \div 9$

5) $63 \div 9$

6) $36 \div 9$

7) $45 \div 9$

8) $45 \div 9$

9) $72 \div 9$

10) $36 \div 9$

11) $54 \div 9$

12) $36 \div 9$

13) $81 \div 9$

14) $36 \div 9$

15) $45 \div 9$

16) $54 \div 9$

17) $45 \div 9$

18) $45 \div 9$

19) $36 \div 9$

20) $63 \div 9$

21) $36 \div 9$

22) $72 \div 9$

23) $36 \div 9$

24) $81 \div 9$

25) $54 \div 9$

26) $63 \div 9$

27) $63 \div 9$

28) $81 \div 9$

29) $27 \div 9$

30) $63 \div 9$

31) $36 \div 9$

32) $36 \div 9$

33) $27 \div 9$

34) $81 \div 9$

35) $9 \div 9$

Let's Divide By 9

Date: ___ Name: ___ Score: ___

1) $54 \div 9$

2) $54 \div 9$

3) $9 \div 9$

4) $27 \div 9$

5) $72 \div 9$

6) $90 \div 9$

7) $72 \div 9$

8) $27 \div 9$

9) $54 \div 9$

10) $90 \div 9$

11) $27 \div 9$

12) $63 \div 9$

13) $54 \div 9$

14) $18 \div 9$

15) $72 \div 9$

16) $90 \div 9$

17) $63 \div 9$

18) $72 \div 9$

19) $63 \div 9$

20) $27 \div 9$

21) $54 \div 9$

22) $81 \div 9$

23) $81 \div 9$

24) $9 \div 9$

25) $72 \div 9$

26) $27 \div 9$

27) $18 \div 9$

28) $90 \div 9$

29) $9 \div 9$

30) $9 \div 9$

31) $18 \div 9$

32) $27 \div 9$

33) $36 \div 9$

34) $90 \div 9$

35) $90 \div 9$

Let's Divide By 9

Date: ___ Name: ___ Score: ___

1) 54 ÷ 9
2) 54 ÷ 9
3) 9 ÷ 9
4) 27 ÷ 9
5) 72 ÷ 9
6) 90 ÷ 9
7) 72 ÷ 9
8) 27 ÷ 9
9) 54 ÷ 9
10) 90 ÷ 9
11) 27 ÷ 9
12) 63 ÷ 9
13) 54 ÷ 9
14) 18 ÷ 9
15) 72 ÷ 9
16) 90 ÷ 9
17) 63 ÷ 9
18) 72 ÷ 9
19) 63 ÷ 9
20) 27 ÷ 9
21) 54 ÷ 9
22) 81 ÷ 9
23) 81 ÷ 9
24) 9 ÷ 9
25) 72 ÷ 9
26) 27 ÷ 9
27) 18 ÷ 9
28) 90 ÷ 9
29) 9 ÷ 9
30) 9 ÷ 9
31) 18 ÷ 9
32) 27 ÷ 9
33) 36 ÷ 9
34) 90 ÷ 9
35) 90 ÷ 9

Page 85

Let's Divide By 9

1) $90 \div 9$

2) $54 \div 9$

3) $90 \div 9$

4) $63 \div 9$

5) $27 \div 9$

6) $54 \div 9$

7) $45 \div 9$

8) $27 \div 9$

9) $18 \div 9$

10) $27 \div 9$

11) $63 \div 9$

12) $72 \div 9$

13) $63 \div 9$

14) $18 \div 9$

15) $90 \div 9$

16) $90 \div 9$

17) $36 \div 9$

18) $90 \div 9$

19) $18 \div 9$

20) $9 \div 9$

21) $27 \div 9$

22) $36 \div 9$

23) $36 \div 9$

24) $9 \div 9$

25) $54 \div 9$

26) $45 \div 9$

27) $27 \div 9$

28) $81 \div 9$

29) $90 \div 9$

30) $9 \div 9$

31) $45 \div 9$

32) $18 \div 9$

33) $72 \div 9$

34) $36 \div 9$

35) $81 \div 9$

Let's Divide By 10

1) $30 \div 10$

2) $90 \div 10$

3) $80 \div 10$

4) $30 \div 10$

5) $70 \div 10$

6) $40 \div 10$

7) $60 \div 10$

8) $70 \div 10$

9) $30 \div 10$

10) $90 \div 10$

11) $90 \div 10$

12) $10 \div 10$

13) $50 \div 10$

14) $40 \div 10$

15) $50 \div 10$

16) $70 \div 10$

17) $40 \div 10$

18) $80 \div 10$

19) $90 \div 10$

20) $70 \div 10$

21) $30 \div 10$

22) $60 \div 10$

23) $60 \div 10$

24) $10 \div 10$

25) $40 \div 10$

26) $20 \div 10$

27) $80 \div 10$

28) $80 \div 10$

29) $60 \div 10$

30) $30 \div 10$

31) $20 \div 10$

32) $40 \div 10$

33) $80 \div 10$

34) $70 \div 10$

35) $50 \div 10$

Let's Divide By 10

1) $70 \div 10$

2) $70 \div 10$

3) $70 \div 10$

4) $90 \div 10$

5) $90 \div 10$

6) $80 \div 10$

7) $10 \div 10$

8) $30 \div 10$

9) $90 \div 10$

10) $30 \div 10$

11) $30 \div 10$

12) $50 \div 10$

13) $60 \div 10$

14) $10 \div 10$

15) $10 \div 10$

16) $40 \div 10$

17) $50 \div 10$

18) $10 \div 10$

19) $60 \div 10$

20) $20 \div 10$

21) $40 \div 10$

22) $60 \div 10$

23) $10 \div 10$

24) $90 \div 10$

25) $20 \div 10$

26) $40 \div 10$

27) $90 \div 10$

28) $40 \div 10$

29) $40 \div 10$

30) $20 \div 10$

31) $50 \div 10$

32) $20 \div 10$

33) $40 \div 10$

34) $90 \div 10$

35) $90 \div 10$

Let's Divide By 10

1) 80 ÷ 10

2) 60 ÷ 10

3) 60 ÷ 10

4) 10 ÷ 10

5) 50 ÷ 10

6) 70 ÷ 10

7) 40 ÷ 10

8) 80 ÷ 10

9) 40 ÷ 10

10) 60 ÷ 10

11) 20 ÷ 10

12) 30 ÷ 10

13) 80 ÷ 10

14) 70 ÷ 10

15) 80 ÷ 10

16) 80 ÷ 10

17) 20 ÷ 10

18) 70 ÷ 10

19) 30 ÷ 10

20) 30 ÷ 10

21) 80 ÷ 10

22) 50 ÷ 10

23) 80 ÷ 10

24) 70 ÷ 10

25) 70 ÷ 10

26) 20 ÷ 10

27) 30 ÷ 10

28) 10 ÷ 10

29) 10 ÷ 10

30) 50 ÷ 10

31) 80 ÷ 10

32) 60 ÷ 10

33) 70 ÷ 10

34) 10 ÷ 10

35) 60 ÷ 10

Let's Divide By 10

1) $\dfrac{70}{\div 10}$

2) $\dfrac{60}{\div 10}$

3) $\dfrac{90}{\div 10}$

4) $\dfrac{50}{\div 10}$

5) $\dfrac{60}{\div 10}$

6) $\dfrac{20}{\div 10}$

7) $\dfrac{50}{\div 10}$

8) $\dfrac{40}{\div 10}$

9) $\dfrac{90}{\div 10}$

10) $\dfrac{60}{\div 10}$

11) $\dfrac{40}{\div 10}$

12) $\dfrac{50}{\div 10}$

13) $\dfrac{10}{\div 10}$

14) $\dfrac{70}{\div 10}$

15) $\dfrac{40}{\div 10}$

16) $\dfrac{40}{\div 10}$

17) $\dfrac{20}{\div 10}$

18) $\dfrac{60}{\div 10}$

19) $\dfrac{30}{\div 10}$

20) $\dfrac{40}{\div 10}$

21) $\dfrac{10}{\div 10}$

22) $\dfrac{70}{\div 10}$

23) $\dfrac{40}{\div 10}$

24) $\dfrac{90}{\div 10}$

25) $\dfrac{50}{\div 10}$

26) $\dfrac{60}{\div 10}$

27) $\dfrac{20}{\div 10}$

28) $\dfrac{10}{\div 10}$

29) $\dfrac{30}{\div 10}$

30) $\dfrac{50}{\div 10}$

31) $\dfrac{90}{\div 10}$

32) $\dfrac{10}{\div 10}$

33) $\dfrac{90}{\div 10}$

34) $\dfrac{80}{\div 10}$

35) $\dfrac{90}{\div 10}$

Let's Divide By 11 & 12

1) $96 \div 12$

2) $36 \div 12$

3) $36 \div 12$

4) $96 \div 12$

5) $99 \div 11$

6) $72 \div 12$

7) $99 \div 11$

8) $36 \div 12$

9) $22 \div 11$

10) $66 \div 11$

11) $99 \div 11$

12) $60 \div 12$

13) $48 \div 12$

14) $60 \div 12$

15) $22 \div 11$

16) $84 \div 12$

17) $12 \div 12$

18) $72 \div 12$

19) $24 \div 12$

20) $72 \div 12$

21) $11 \div 11$

22) $36 \div 12$

23) $77 \div 11$

24) $55 \div 11$

25) $24 \div 12$

26) $55 \div 11$

27) $99 \div 11$

28) $96 \div 12$

29) $72 \div 12$

30) $60 \div 12$

31) $22 \div 11$

32) $48 \div 12$

33) $84 \div 12$

34) $66 \div 11$

35) $77 \div 11$

Let's Divide By 11 & 12

1) 60 ÷ 12

2) 99 ÷ 11

3) 60 ÷ 12

4) 60 ÷ 12

5) 48 ÷ 12

6) 48 ÷ 12

7) 96 ÷ 12

8) 33 ÷ 11

9) 48 ÷ 12

10) 24 ÷ 12

11) 48 ÷ 12

12) 48 ÷ 12

13) 44 ÷ 11

14) 84 ÷ 12

15) 11 ÷ 11

16) 33 ÷ 11

17) 22 ÷ 11

18) 22 ÷ 11

19) 11 ÷ 11

20) 24 ÷ 12

21) 11 ÷ 11

22) 77 ÷ 11

23) 72 ÷ 12

24) 33 ÷ 11

25) 48 ÷ 12

26) 88 ÷ 11

27) 77 ÷ 11

28) 88 ÷ 11

29) 48 ÷ 12

30) 77 ÷ 11

31) 48 ÷ 12

32) 48 ÷ 12

33) 96 ÷ 12

34) 12 ÷ 12

35) 66 ÷ 11

Date: Name: Score:

Let's Divide By 11 & 12

1) $11 \div 11$

2) $22 \div 11$

3) $11 \div 11$

4) $72 \div 12$

5) $24 \div 12$

6) $24 \div 12$

7) $24 \div 12$

8) $66 \div 11$

9) $33 \div 11$

10) $33 \div 11$

11) $44 \div 11$

12) $55 \div 11$

13) $72 \div 12$

14) $99 \div 11$

15) $72 \div 12$

16) $96 \div 12$

17) $66 \div 11$

18) $66 \div 11$

19) $77 \div 11$

20) $88 \div 11$

21) $77 \div 11$

22) $44 \div 11$

23) $84 \div 12$

24) $33 \div 11$

25) $36 \div 12$

26) $99 \div 11$

27) $60 \div 12$

28) $48 \div 12$

29) $12 \div 12$

30) $44 \div 11$

31) $60 \div 12$

32) $22 \div 11$

33) $22 \div 11$

34) $96 \div 12$

35) $48 \div 12$

Let's Divide By 11 & 12

1) $\begin{array}{r} 44 \\ \div\ 11 \end{array}$

2) $\begin{array}{r} 55 \\ \div\ 11 \end{array}$

3) $\begin{array}{r} 22 \\ \div\ 11 \end{array}$

4) $\begin{array}{r} 77 \\ \div\ 11 \end{array}$

5) $\begin{array}{r} 33 \\ \div\ 11 \end{array}$

6) $\begin{array}{r} 88 \\ \div\ 11 \end{array}$

7) $\begin{array}{r} 72 \\ \div\ 12 \end{array}$

8) $\begin{array}{r} 55 \\ \div\ 11 \end{array}$

9) $\begin{array}{r} 44 \\ \div\ 11 \end{array}$

10) $\begin{array}{r} 33 \\ \div\ 11 \end{array}$

11) $\begin{array}{r} 44 \\ \div\ 11 \end{array}$

12) $\begin{array}{r} 55 \\ \div\ 11 \end{array}$

13) $\begin{array}{r} 44 \\ \div\ 11 \end{array}$

14) $\begin{array}{r} 24 \\ \div\ 12 \end{array}$

15) $\begin{array}{r} 48 \\ \div\ 12 \end{array}$

16) $\begin{array}{r} 24 \\ \div\ 12 \end{array}$

17) $\begin{array}{r} 72 \\ \div\ 12 \end{array}$

18) $\begin{array}{r} 60 \\ \div\ 12 \end{array}$

19) $\begin{array}{r} 24 \\ \div\ 12 \end{array}$

20) $\begin{array}{r} 99 \\ \div\ 11 \end{array}$

21) $\begin{array}{r} 72 \\ \div\ 12 \end{array}$

22) $\begin{array}{r} 96 \\ \div\ 12 \end{array}$

23) $\begin{array}{r} 48 \\ \div\ 12 \end{array}$

24) $\begin{array}{r} 99 \\ \div\ 11 \end{array}$

25) $\begin{array}{r} 36 \\ \div\ 12 \end{array}$

26) $\begin{array}{r} 84 \\ \div\ 12 \end{array}$

27) $\begin{array}{r} 24 \\ \div\ 12 \end{array}$

28) $\begin{array}{r} 96 \\ \div\ 12 \end{array}$

29) $\begin{array}{r} 33 \\ \div\ 11 \end{array}$

30) $\begin{array}{r} 55 \\ \div\ 11 \end{array}$

31) $\begin{array}{r} 77 \\ \div\ 11 \end{array}$

32) $\begin{array}{r} 44 \\ \div\ 11 \end{array}$

33) $\begin{array}{r} 22 \\ \div\ 11 \end{array}$

34) $\begin{array}{r} 12 \\ \div\ 12 \end{array}$

35) $\begin{array}{r} 66 \\ \div\ 11 \end{array}$

Mixed Division 0-12

1) $64 \div 0$

2) $98 \div 2$

3) $54 \div 6$

4) $12 \div 3$

5) $91 \div 7$

6) $3 \div 1$

7) $11 \div 1$

8) $31 \div 1$

9) $77 \div 11$

10) $7 \div 7$

11) $67 \div 1$

12) $57 \div 3$

13) $54 \div 9$

14) $39 \div 1$

15) $53 \div 1$

16) $49 \div 7$

17) $19 \div 1$

18) $42 \div 1$

19) $54 \div 2$

20) $46 \div 2$

21) $79 \div 1$

22) $84 \div 1$

23) $76 \div 2$

24) $74 \div 2$

25) $72 \div 4$

26) $93 \div 1$

27) $79 \div 1$

28) $6 \div 0$

29) $68 \div 0$

30) $89 \div 1$

31) $3 \div 3$

32) $15 \div 3$

33) $34 \div 2$

34) $59 \div 1$

35) $70 \div 2$

Mixed Division 0-12

1) $96 \div 12$

2) $99 \div 1$

3) $71 \div 1$

4) $29 \div 1$

5) $82 \div 2$

6) $28 \div 7$

7) $5 \div 5$

8) $64 \div 0$

9) $56 \div 2$

10) $59 \div 1$

11) $4 \div 1$

12) $65 \div 0$

13) $94 \div 1$

14) $92 \div 4$

15) $28 \div 4$

16) $89 \div 1$

17) $83 \div 1$

18) $31 \div 1$

19) $78 \div 6$

20) $75 \div 1$

21) $31 \div 1$

22) $19 \div 0$

23) $1 \div 1$

24) $9 \div 9$

25) $50 \div 5$

26) $62 \div 2$

27) $77 \div 7$

28) $16 \div 2$

29) $17 \div 1$

30) $65 \div 5$

31) $27 \div 1$

32) $15 \div 5$

33) $21 \div 7$

34) $33 \div 3$

35) $72 \div 1$

Mixed Division 0-12

1) $44 \div 11$

2) $47 \div 1$

3) $26 \div 1$

4) $27 \div 1$

5) $34 \div 2$

6) $20 \div 0$

7) $35 \div 5$

8) $5 \div 5$

9) $51 \div 1$

10) $42 \div 2$

11) $44 \div 1$

12) $19 \div 1$

13) $72 \div 12$

14) $75 \div 5$

15) $33 \div 11$

16) $9 \div 1$

17) $75 \div 1$

18) $74 \div 1$

19) $28 \div 0$

20) $48 \div 6$

21) $8 \div 1$

22) $67 \div 1$

23) $78 \div 6$

24) $28 \div 2$

25) $14 \div 2$

26) $71 \div 1$

27) $33 \div 1$

28) $22 \div 1$

29) $22 \div 0$

30) $16 \div 2$

31) $75 \div 3$

32) $43 \div 1$

33) $68 \div 2$

34) $50 \div 2$

35) $22 \div 2$

Mixed Division 0-12

1) $38 \div 2$

2) $23 \div 1$

3) $78 \div 3$

4) $16 \div 1$

5) $51 \div 3$

6) $32 \div 8$

7) $31 \div 1$

8) $87 \div 3$

9) $32 \div 1$

10) $34 \div 2$

11) $7 \div 7$

12) $75 \div 1$

13) $75 \div 1$

14) $42 \div 7$

15) $14 \div 7$

16) $21 \div 7$

17) $76 \div 4$

18) $87 \div 3$

19) $63 \div 1$

20) $52 \div 1$

21) $4 \div 2$

22) $39 \div 3$

23) $86 \div 1$

24) $91 \div 7$

25) $33 \div 1$

26) $78 \div 1$

27) $72 \div 12$

28) $76 \div 2$

29) $85 \div 1$

30) $80 \div 1$

31) $10 \div 2$

32) $87 \div 3$

33) $60 \div 2$

34) $4 \div 2$

35) $45 \div 5$

Mixed Division 0-12

1)
$$19 \div 1$$

2)
$$16 \div 1$$

3)
$$84 \div 3$$

4)
$$73 \div 1$$

5)
$$96 \div 1$$

6)
$$41 \div 1$$

7)
$$43 \div 1$$

8)
$$21 \div 3$$

9)
$$95 \div 1$$

10)
$$32 \div 1$$

11)
$$50 \div 10$$

12)
$$43 \div 1$$

13)
$$97 \div 1$$

14)
$$18 \div 2$$

15)
$$61 \div 1$$

16)
$$35 \div 1$$

17)
$$83 \div 1$$

18)
$$38 \div 2$$

19)
$$13 \div 1$$

20)
$$36 \div 12$$

21)
$$1 \div 1$$

22)
$$12 \div 1$$

23)
$$76 \div 2$$

24)
$$82 \div 2$$

25)
$$43 \div 1$$

26)
$$58 \div 1$$

27)
$$68 \div 2$$

28)
$$8 \div 2$$

29)
$$13 \div 1$$

30)
$$2 \div 1$$

31)
$$49 \div 1$$

32)
$$29 \div 1$$

33)
$$82 \div 2$$

34)
$$45 \div 3$$

35)
$$68 \div 4$$

Mixed Division 0-12

1) 13 ÷ 1

2) 4 ÷ 4

3) 71 ÷ 1

4) 56 ÷ 7

5) 47 ÷ 1

6) 1 ÷ 1

7) 95 ÷ 1

8) 78 ÷ 3

9) 26 ÷ 1

10) 45 ÷ 5

11) 74 ÷ 1

12) 54 ÷ 1

13) 91 ÷ 7

14) 48 ÷ 2

15) 23 ÷ 1

16) 43 ÷ 1

17) 30 ÷ 6

18) 47 ÷ 1

19) 47 ÷ 1

20) 7 ÷ 7

21) 93 ÷ 1

22) 65 ÷ 1

23) 65 ÷ 5

24) 47 ÷ 1

25) 81 ÷ 3

26) 41 ÷ 1

27) 26 ÷ 1

28) 1 ÷ 1

29) 72 ÷ 8

30) 34 ÷ 2

31) 27 ÷ 9

32) 79 ÷ 1

33) 46 ÷ 2

34) 47 ÷ 1

35) 22 ÷ 11

PART 3:

SOLUTIONS

Solutions:

Multiplication & Division

Page 1, Item 1:
(1)0 (2)0 (3)0 (4)0 (5)5 (6)3 (7)0 (8)3 (9)1
(10)0 (11)0 (12)3 (13)7 (14)0 (15)2

Page 1, Item 2:
(16)2 (17)4 (18)5 (19)0 (20)4 (21)0 (22)0
(23)7 (24)0 (25)0 (26)7 (27)5 (28)0 (29)0
(30)2 (31)0 (32)0 (33)0 (34)0 (35)0

Page 2, Item 1:
(1)6 (2)7 (3)0 (4)3 (5)0 (6)8 (7)0 (8)1 (9)6
(10)4 (11)0 (12)0 (13)0 (14)0 (15)6

Page 2, Item 2:
(16)1 (17)5 (18)0 (19)6 (20)1 (21)8 (22)0
(23)8 (24)0 (25)1 (26)0 (27)6 (28)0 (29)3
(30)0 (31)0 (32)0 (33)4 (34)0 (35)0

Page 3, Item 1:
(1)6 (2)3 (3)0 (4)0 (5)4 (6)0 (7)7 (8)0 (9)0
(10)2 (11)0 (12)0 (13)9 (14)1 (15)4

Page 3, Item 2:
(16)0 (17)0 (18)0 (19)0 (20)0 (21)0 (22)0
(23)3 (24)9 (25)0 (26)4 (27)0 (28)0 (29)7
(30)4 (31)0 (32)0 (33)6 (34)0 (35)9

Page 4, Item 1:
(1)0 (2)0 (3)7 (4)0 (5)0 (6)3 (7)1 (8)0 (9)0
(10)0 (11)0 (12)5 (13)5 (14)0 (15)0

Page 4, Item 2:
(16)2 (17)8 (18)0 (19)0 (20)8 (21)0 (22)6
(23)0 (24)0 (25)8 (26)0 (27)0 (28)0 (29)6
(30)4 (31)0 (32)0 (33)0 (34)2 (35)0

Page 5, Item 1:
(1)12 (2)18 (3)10 (4)6 (5)2 (6)14 (7)2
(8)18 (9)14 (10)12 (11)6 (12)12 (13)2
(14)14 (15)0

Page 5, Item 2:
(16)6 (17)16 (18)4 (19)4 (20)2 (21)2
(22)14 (23)10 (24)6 (25)2 (26)2 (27)8
(28)8 (29)12 (30)4 (31)2 (32)10 (33)4
(34)16 (35)10

Page 6, Item 1:
(1)2 (2)6 (3)18 (4)10 (5)10 (6)18 (7)8 (8)0
(9)6 (10)12 (11)8 (12)18 (13)16 (14)14
(15)8

Page 6, Item 2:
(16)18 (17)14 (18)16 (19)14 (20)2 (21)14
(22)14 (23)14 (24)18 (25)0 (26)12 (27)14
(28)6 (29)16 (30)14 (31)10 (32)6 (33)6
(34)12 (35)8

Page 7, Item 1:
(1)2 (2)16 (3)16 (4)14 (5)2 (6)0 (7)6 (8)14
(9)12 (10)6 (11)6 (12)12 (13)16 (14)14
(15)8

Page 7, Item 2:
(16)16 (17)18 (18)8 (19)0 (20)8 (21)12
(22)4 (23)4 (24)6 (25)16 (26)8 (27)6
(28)14 (29)16 (30)16 (31)2 (32)10 (33)12
(34)0 (35)18

Page 8, Item 1:
(1)6 (2)10 (3)8 (4)8 (5)2 (6)10 (7)8 (8)18
(9)16 (10)10 (11)18 (12)16 (13)4 (14)6
(15)8

Page 8, Item 2:
(16)4 (17)6 (18)14 (19)0 (20)4 (21)12
(22)4 (23)4 (24)14 (25)16 (26)16 (27)18
(28)6 (29)4 (30)16 (31)14 (32)18 (33)12
(34)8 (35)2

Page 9, Item 1:
(1)27 (2)6 (3)6 (4)27 (5)15 (6)18 (7)24
(8)21 (9)27 (10)9 (11)9 (12)3 (13)12

(14)27 (15)12

Page 9, Item 2:
(16)0 (17)18 (18)21 (19)24 (20)15 (21)15
(22)6 (23)15 (24)18 (25)24 (26)15 (27)21
(28)3 (29)21 (30)12 (31)18 (32)15 (33)6
(34)9 (35)9

Page 10, Item 1:
(1)18 (2)27 (3)21 (4)9 (5)21 (6)24 (7)3
(8)18 (9)27 (10)27 (11)21 (12)27 (13)27
(14)18 (15)18

Page 10, Item 2:
(16)0 (17)27 (18)18 (19)12 (20)3 (21)9
(22)6 (23)15 (24)3 (25)12 (26)24 (27)9
(28)27 (29)6 (30)9 (31)18 (32)9 (33)6
(34)18 (35)15

Page 11, Item 1:
(1)9 (2)27 (3)9 (4)3 (5)24 (6)6 (7)24 (8)6
(9)18 (10)12 (11)18 (12)15 (13)12 (14)9
(15)0

Page 11, Item 2:
(16)15 (17)27 (18)27 (19)9 (20)6 (21)24
(22)9 (23)12 (24)27 (25)18 (26)21 (27)27
(28)12 (29)0 (30)18 (31)12 (32)18 (33)9
(34)27 (35)21

Page 12, Item 1:
(1)27 (2)12 (3)6 (4)21 (5)27 (6)18 (7)27
(8)15 (9)0 (10)0 (11)24 (12)0 (13)27
(14)21 (15)6

Page 12, Item 2:
(16)3 (17)21 (18)21 (19)21 (20)18 (21)3
(22)0 (23)12 (24)15 (25)12 (26)24 (27)27
(28)24 (29)24 (30)9 (31)27 (32)21 (33)18
(34)0 (35)0

Page 13, Item 1:
(1)12 (2)24 (3)36 (4)0 (5)16 (6)20 (7)28
(8)20 (9)4 (10)0 (11)36 (12)20 (13)20
(14)16 (15)20

Page 13, Item 2:
(16)0 (17)32 (18)32 (19)24 (20)28 (21)20
(22)0 (23)8 (24)36 (25)12 (26)12 (27)16
(28)20 (29)32 (30)36 (31)0 (32)28 (33)36
(34)20 (35)20

Page 14, Item 1:
(1)16 (2)24 (3)24 (4)24 (5)16 (6)24 (7)12
(8)20 (9)8 (10)32 (11)0 (12)24 (13)20
(14)28 (15)20

Page 14, Item 2:
(16)24 (17)28 (18)8 (19)8 (20)28 (21)36
(22)16 (23)12 (24)12 (25)36 (26)0 (27)4
(28)16 (29)20 (30)0 (31)24 (32)4 (33)16
(34)24 (35)32

Page 15, Item 1:
(1)16 (2)0 (3)4 (4)36 (5)4 (6)32 (7)28
(8)32 (9)12 (10)28 (11)12 (12)24 (13)28
(14)24 (15)32

Page 15, Item 2:
(16)4 (17)0 (18)32 (19)8 (20)16 (21)0
(22)0 (23)20 (24)28 (25)12 (26)36 (27)20
(28)12 (29)4 (30)0 (31)32 (32)16 (33)12
(34)20 (35)4

Page 16, Item 1:
(1)12 (2)28 (3)12 (4)8 (5)20 (6)4 (7)20
(8)32 (9)20 (10)16 (11)12 (12)36 (13)24
(14)12 (15)32

Page 16, Item 2:
(16)8 (17)20 (18)24 (19)0 (20)20 (21)8
(22)32 (23)32 (24)36 (25)12 (26)36 (27)16

(28)20 (29)20 (30)16 (31)4 (32)28 (33)24 (34)4 (35)12

Page 17, Item 1:
(1)20 (2)45 (3)45 (4)15 (5)35 (6)35 (7)30 (8)30 (9)10 (10)40 (11)15 (12)40 (13)15 (14)40 (15)45

Page 17, Item 2:
(16)35 (17)15 (18)15 (19)35 (20)25 (21)0 (22)40 (23)10 (24)0 (25)35 (26)35 (27)20 (28)10 (29)30 (30)5 (31)40 (32)35 (33)45 (34)25 (35)20

Page 18, Item 1:
(1)30 (2)5 (3)25 (4)15 (5)20 (6)40 (7)35 (8)10 (9)35 (10)10 (11)10 (12)45 (13)5 (14)5 (15)25

Page 18, Item 2:
(16)25 (17)35 (18)35 (19)20 (20)10 (21)25 (22)30 (23)10 (24)25 (25)15 (26)10 (27)15 (28)15 (29)25 (30)10 (31)45 (32)0 (33)35 (34)15 (35)25

Page 19, Item 1:
(1)30 (2)30 (3)10 (4)25 (5)15 (6)15 (7)15 (8)5 (9)30 (10)35 (11)10 (12)35 (13)20 (14)15 (15)35

Page 19, Item 2:
(16)5 (17)30 (18)10 (19)15 (20)0 (21)15 (22)35 (23)30 (24)10 (25)15 (26)10 (27)25 (28)45 (29)30 (30)10 (31)25 (32)10 (33)30 (34)15 (35)25

Page 20, Item 1:
(1)40 (2)10 (3)45 (4)30 (5)30 (6)15 (7)45 (8)25 (9)30 (10)35 (11)10 (12)20 (13)25 (14)15 (15)30

Page 20, Item 2:
(16)10 (17)40 (18)25 (19)20 (20)20 (21)10 (22)0 (23)10 (24)30 (25)45 (26)20 (27)25 (28)10 (29)10 (30)30 (31)15 (32)0 (33)10

(34)35 (35)25

Page 21, Item 1:
(1)12 (2)42 (3)24 (4)48 (5)12 (6)12 (7)12 (8)12 (9)18 (10)18 (11)24 (12)42 (13)24 (14)42 (15)36

Page 21, Item 2:
(16)36 (17)30 (18)36 (19)12 (20)48 (21)36 (22)6 (23)42 (24)24 (25)6 (26)12 (27)54 (28)42 (29)12 (30)36 (31)12 (32)48 (33)36 (34)48 (35)42

Page 22, Item 1:
(1)24 (2)54 (3)30 (4)36 (5)0 (6)12 (7)6 (8)0 (9)48 (10)24 (11)36 (12)24 (13)42 (14)54 (15)48

Page 22, Item 2:
(16)54 (17)24 (18)24 (19)12 (20)30 (21)24 (22)36 (23)18 (24)18 (25)48 (26)6 (27)12 (28)12 (29)6 (30)12 (31)24 (32)54 (33)48 (34)36 (35)18

Page 23, Item 1:
(1)6 (2)12 (3)18 (4)6 (5)42 (6)18 (7)54 (8)18 (9)0 (10)24 (11)18 (12)48 (13)42 (14)30 (15)0

Page 23, Item 2:
(16)48 (17)6 (18)54 (19)54 (20)36 (21)0 (22)24 (23)18 (24)6 (25)54 (26)18 (27)42 (28)0 (29)12 (30)54 (31)0 (32)42 (33)48 (34)36 (35)18

Page 24, Item 1:
(1)18 (2)0 (3)6 (4)0 (5)48 (6)48 (7)54 (8)36 (9)24 (10)6 (11)6 (12)24 (13)0 (14)30

(15)54

Page 24, Item 2:
(16)54 (17)42 (18)42 (19)42 (20)54 (21)12
(22)12 (23)12 (24)42 (25)6 (26)24 (27)12
(28)42 (29)36 (30)54 (31)18 (32)42 (33)36
(34)18 (35)36

Page 25, Item 1:
(1)0 (2)56 (3)7 (4)21 (5)63 (6)21 (7)7
(8)35 (9)63 (10)7 (11)56 (12)56 (13)63
(14)49 (15)35

Page 25, Item 2:
(16)0 (17)7 (18)63 (19)35 (20)28 (21)0
(22)63 (23)7 (24)49 (25)63 (26)21 (27)56
(28)63 (29)28 (30)28 (31)49 (32)21 (33)56
(34)0 (35)42

Page 26, Item 1:
(1)7 (2)42 (3)49 (4)63 (5)42 (6)28 (7)56
(8)42 (9)28 (10)7 (11)14 (12)35 (13)7
(14)49 (15)49

Page 26, Item 2:
(16)14 (17)49 (18)21 (19)28 (20)21 (21)35
(22)21 (23)56 (24)35 (25)14 (26)0 (27)7
(28)21 (29)28 (30)21 (31)63 (32)14 (33)56
(34)0 (35)7

Page 27, Item 1:
(1)49 (2)0 (3)49 (4)7 (5)63 (6)21 (7)28
(8)14 (9)28 (10)0 (11)63 (12)49 (13)42
(14)7 (15)35

Page 27, Item 2:
(16)63 (17)0 (18)42 (19)56 (20)49 (21)35
(22)35 (23)7 (24)63 (25)21 (26)28 (27)21
(28)7 (29)0 (30)56 (31)35 (32)14 (33)35
(34)42 (35)0

Page 28, Item 1:
(1)42 (2)63 (3)28 (4)63 (5)7 (6)0 (7)35
(8)21 (9)0 (10)14 (11)35 (12)35 (13)63
(14)49 (15)28

Page 28, Item 2:
(16)56 (17)7 (18)63 (19)35 (20)7 (21)21
(22)42 (23)28 (24)7 (25)49 (26)7 (27)28
(28)56 (29)49 (30)42 (31)14 (32)42 (33)28
(34)35 (35)0

Page 29, Item 1:
(1)24 (2)56 (3)32 (4)32 (5)8 (6)16 (7)64
(8)8 (9)40 (10)64 (11)0 (12)40 (13)40
(14)72 (15)40

Page 29, Item 2:
(16)8 (17)8 (18)16 (19)64 (20)0 (21)24
(22)64 (23)32 (24)16 (25)40 (26)24 (27)56
(28)32 (29)64 (30)56 (31)0 (32)72 (33)32
(34)16 (35)24

Page 30, Item 1:
(1)8 (2)56 (3)56 (4)32 (5)8 (6)0 (7)0 (8)56
(9)72 (10)32 (11)24 (12)8 (13)32 (14)32
(15)8

Page 30, Item 2:
(16)32 (17)64 (18)40 (19)40 (20)8 (21)16
(22)8 (23)72 (24)48 (25)48 (26)40 (27)48
(28)0 (29)0 (30)72 (31)24 (32)24 (33)56
(34)56 (35)48

Page 31, Item 1:
(1)72 (2)48 (3)16 (4)24 (5)40 (6)48 (7)24
(8)16 (9)48 (10)56 (11)48 (12)16 (13)24
(14)0 (15)40

Page 31, Item 2:
(16)0 (17)0 (18)64 (19)32 (20)40 (21)16
(22)16 (23)64 (24)32 (25)72 (26)8 (27)40

(28)0 (29)8 (30)56 (31)72 (32)72 (33)0
(34)24 (35)48

Page 32, Item 1:
(1)16 (2)72 (3)16 (4)56 (5)64 (6)72 (7)8
(8)16 (9)64 (10)32 (11)32 (12)48 (13)0
(14)56 (15)64

Page 32, Item 2:
(16)8 (17)64 (18)24 (19)8 (20)40 (21)56
(22)72 (23)8 (24)48 (25)64 (26)32 (27)56
(28)16 (29)8 (30)48 (31)24 (32)0 (33)24
(34)56 (35)0

Page 33, Item 1:
(1)81 (2)27 (3)45 (4)36 (5)45 (6)9 (7)0
(8)27 (9)45 (10)81 (11)18 (12)9 (13)63
(14)27 (15)36

Page 33, Item 2:
(16)36 (17)54 (18)63 (19)45 (20)63 (21)0
(22)18 (23)72 (24)72 (25)9 (26)81 (27)54
(28)45 (29)72 (30)45 (31)9 (32)36 (33)36
(34)18 (35)18

Page 34, Item 1:
(1)45 (2)18 (3)27 (4)18 (5)9 (6)54 (7)63
(8)54 (9)9 (10)36 (11)0 (12)54 (13)9 (14)0
(15)54

Page 34, Item 2:
(16)36 (17)9 (18)27 (19)72 (20)45 (21)63
(22)18 (23)63 (24)27 (25)54 (26)81 (27)54
(28)63 (29)27 (30)72 (31)45 (32)9 (33)27
(34)0 (35)18

Page 35, Item 1:
(1)72 (2)63 (3)63 (4)0 (5)18 (6)36 (7)72
(8)81 (9)36 (10)45 (11)72 (12)18 (13)81
(14)72 (15)27

Page 35, Item 2:
(16)9 (17)9 (18)27 (19)81 (20)18 (21)0
(22)27 (23)18 (24)0 (25)63 (26)72 (27)45
(28)0 (29)54 (30)0 (31)18 (32)27 (33)63

(34)45 (35)54

Page 36, Item 1:
(1)54 (2)63 (3)27 (4)18 (5)27 (6)72 (7)27
(8)45 (9)54 (10)54 (11)72 (12)0 (13)0
(14)36 (15)54

Page 36, Item 2:
(16)72 (17)54 (18)36 (19)54 (20)9 (21)36
(22)18 (23)45 (24)18 (25)18 (26)81 (27)18
(28)9 (29)72 (30)72 (31)54 (32)45 (33)0
(34)27 (35)18

Page 37, Item 1:
(1)90 (2)90 (3)50 (4)0 (5)20 (6)30 (7)60
(8)70 (9)90 (10)60 (11)80 (12)60 (13)10
(14)0 (15)50

Page 37, Item 2:
(16)90 (17)20 (18)30 (19)10 (20)80 (21)40
(22)30 (23)30 (24)10 (25)60 (26)10 (27)40
(28)60 (29)40 (30)60 (31)40 (32)70 (33)70
(34)20 (35)0

Page 38, Item 1:
(1)30 (2)30 (3)70 (4)50 (5)60 (6)70 (7)70
(8)90 (9)20 (10)70 (11)0 (12)40 (13)10
(14)10 (15)30

Page 38, Item 2:
(16)70 (17)60 (18)10 (19)80 (20)20 (21)20
(22)40 (23)0 (24)70 (25)30 (26)30 (27)20
(28)10 (29)70 (30)60 (31)60 (32)0 (33)60
(34)60 (35)30

Page 39, Item 1:
(1)30 (2)50 (3)80 (4)60 (5)40 (6)20 (7)30
(8)40 (9)10 (10)0 (11)60 (12)60 (13)60

(14)90 (15)0

Page 39, Item 2:
(16)50 (17)40 (18)70 (19)20 (20)60 (21)0
(22)10 (23)20 (24)70 (25)50 (26)60 (27)0
(28)70 (29)70 (30)70 (31)20 (32)50 (33)90
(34)40 (35)30

Page 40, Item 1:
(1)60 (2)10 (3)30 (4)70 (5)40 (6)20 (7)80
(8)90 (9)50 (10)60 (11)20 (12)0 (13)70
(14)0 (15)50

Page 40, Item 2:
(16)0 (17)90 (18)70 (19)60 (20)20 (21)0
(22)20 (23)50 (24)0 (25)40 (26)20 (27)80
(28)70 (29)60 (30)10 (31)10 (32)50 (33)50
(34)0 (35)80

Page 41, Item 1:
(1)24 (2)24 (3)33 (4)84 (5)55 (6)88 (7)11
(8)99 (9)24 (10)24 (11)12 (12)44 (13)0
(14)99 (15)108

Page 41, Item 2:
(16)33 (17)0 (18)99 (19)99 (20)36 (21)12
(22)72 (23)11 (24)22 (25)44 (26)99 (27)77
(28)88 (29)60 (30)33 (31)44 (32)55 (33)96
(34)96 (35)36

Page 42, Item 1:
(1)44 (2)99 (3)24 (4)0 (5)60 (6)84 (7)11
(8)11 (9)0 (10)72 (11)66 (12)72 (13)44
(14)55 (15)12

Page 42, Item 2:
(16)36 (17)96 (18)88 (19)66 (20)99 (21)84
(22)0 (23)77 (24)99 (25)66 (26)72 (27)0
(28)33 (29)0 (30)99 (31)48 (32)36 (33)77
(34)96 (35)22

Page 43, Item 1:
(1)24 (2)0 (3)22 (4)24 (5)48 (6)96 (7)0
(8)12 (9)84 (10)22 (11)55 (12)77 (13)99
(14)12 (15)96

Page 43, Item 2:
(16)0 (17)96 (18)66 (19)11 (20)12 (21)66
(22)33 (23)96 (24)0 (25)11 (26)108 (27)12
(28)96 (29)12 (30)48 (31)84 (32)66 (33)55
(34)33 (35)60

Page 44, Item 1:
(1)96 (2)84 (3)96 (4)0 (5)0 (6)0 (7)48 (8)0
(9)12 (10)77 (11)72 (12)22 (13)66 (14)108
(15)24

Page 44, Item 2:
(16)99 (17)0 (18)99 (19)12 (20)48 (21)60
(22)48 (23)48 (24)44 (25)55 (26)24 (27)99
(28)24 (29)22 (30)66 (31)44 (32)77 (33)99
(34)36 (35)66

Page 45, Item 1:
(1)56 (2)18 (3)10 (4)0 (5)15 (6)12 (7)48
(8)24 (9)30 (10)60 (11)10 (12)99 (13)10
(14)8 (15)7 (16)10 (17)10 (18)27 (19)32
(20)0 (21)36 (22)63 (23)0 (24)30 (25)6
(26)12 (27)63 (28)60 (29)18 (30)3 (31)80
(32)0 (33)3 (34)6 (35)12

Page 46, Item 1:
(1)84 (2)36 (3)18 (4)96 (5)12 (6)24 (7)30
(8)35 (9)24 (10)49 (11)12 (12)0 (13)45
(14)2 (15)24 (16)54 (17)40 (18)18 (19)10
(20)4 (21)0 (22)30 (23)40 (24)16 (25)0
(26)5 (27)0 (28)70 (29)0 (30)99 (31)60
(32)4 (33)3 (34)0 (35)56

Page 47, Item 1:
(1)21 (2)35 (3)27 (4)36 (5)24 (6)15 (7)8
(8)45 (9)18 (10)0 (11)16 (12)7 (13)21
(14)60 (15)32 (16)14 (17)63 (18)18 (19)4
(20)8 (21)12 (22)99 (23)24 (24)42 (25)30
(26)36 (27)24 (28)0 (29)0 (30)18 (31)0
(32)10 (33)0 (34)54 (35)12

Page 48, Item 1:
(1)21 (2)96 (3)0 (4)42 (5)56 (6)0 (7)27
(8)77 (9)99 (10)12 (11)0 (12)36 (13)33
(14)0 (15)0 (16)6 (17)0 (18)40 (19)27
(20)1 (21)24 (22)0 (23)18 (24)3 (25)0
(26)12 (27)40 (28)48 (29)60 (30)28 (31)90
(32)36 (33)0 (34)90 (35)16

Page 49, Item 1:
(1)2 (2)8 (3)3 (4)48 (5)16 (6)2 (7)64 (8)21
(9)60 (10)9 (11)6 (12)14 (13)42 (14)18
(15)8 (16)96 (17)4 (18)6 (19)8 (20)8
(21)45 (22)0 (23)81 (24)16 (25)40 (26)0
(27)24 (28)25 (29)18 (30)36 (31)4 (32)77
(33)8 (34)108 (35)64

Page 50, Item 1:
(1)24 (2)0 (3)16 (4)81 (5)0 (6)0 (7)21 (8)8
(9)9 (10)40 (11)35 (12)35 (13)0 (14)30

(15)0 (16)81 (17)12 (18)42 (19)20 (20)49
(21)10 (22)8 (23)8 (24)81 (25)36 (26)18
(27)11 (28)36 (29)0 (30)55 (31)56 (32)27
(33)40 (34)72 (35)9

Page 51, Item 1:
(1)2 (2)∞ (3)2 (4)7 (5)5 (6)∞ (7)6 (8)3
(9)7 (10)10 (11)2 (12)7 (13)6 (14)6 (15)1
(16)6 (17)∞ (18)6 (19)4 (20)9 (21)9 (22)4
(23)7 (24)8 (25)6 (26)8 (27)10 (28)3
(29)10 (30)1 (31)8 (32)5 (33)4 (34)9 (35)4

Page 52, Item 1:
(1)9 (2)1 (3)4 (4)1 (5)7 (6)1 (7)1 (8)5 (9)9
(10)3 (11)3 (12)1 (13)6 (14)7 (15)10 (16)8
(17)2 (18)2 (19)∞ (20)8 (21)5 (22)8
(23)∞ (24)6 (25)1 (26)3 (27)∞ (28)6
(29)4 (30)5 (31)7 (32)3 (33)4 (34)1 (35)10

Page 53, Item 1:
(1)10 (2)10 (3)7 (4)7 (5)2 (6)1 (7)8 (8)3
(9)10 (10)1 (11)2 (12)7 (13)3 (14)10 (15)1
(16)4 (17)4 (18)8 (19)1 (20)3 (21)5 (22)∞
(23)9 (24)∞ (25)4 (26)1 (27)1 (28)9
(29)10 (30)3 (31)7 (32)9 (33)6 (34)3
(35)∞

Page 54, Item 1:
(1)5 (2)8 (3)5 (4)7 (5)7 (6)9 (7)3 (8)1 (9)∞
(10)∞ (11)4 (12)6 (13)4 (14)7 (15)2 (16)7
(17)8 (18)8 (19)8 (20)2 (21)4 (22)6 (23)∞
(24)3 (25)5 (26)4 (27)6 (28)2 (29)10 (30)6
(31)5 (32)6 (33)2 (34)3 (35)10

Page 55, Item 1:
(1)2 (2)6 (3)8 (4)7 (5)6 (6)7 (7)10 (8)5
(9)10 (10)8 (11)10 (12)6 (13)8 (14)9
(15)10 (16)2 (17)3 (18)1 (19)6 (20)10
(21)3 (22)3 (23)2 (24)2 (25)9 (26)4 (27)8
(28)3 (29)6 (30)6 (31)5 (32)4 (33)8 (34)3
(35)6

Page 56, Item 1:
(1)8 (2)2 (3)1 (4)9 (5)6 (6)7 (7)7 (8)9 (9)10
(10)2 (11)10 (12)3 (13)9 (14)9 (15)8 (16)7
(17)9 (18)9 (19)8 (20)3 (21)4 (22)9 (23)6
(24)3 (25)7 (26)3 (27)3 (28)7 (29)8 (30)1
(31)8 (32)1 (33)7 (34)3 (35)4

Page 57, Item 1:
(1)9 (2)2 (3)4 (4)8 (5)1 (6)2 (7)7 (8)4 (9)5
(10)10 (11)3 (12)7 (13)4 (14)4 (15)9
(16)10 (17)10 (18)7 (19)6 (20)2 (21)5
(22)2 (23)9 (24)7 (25)9 (26)6 (27)1 (28)4
(29)1 (30)9 (31)2 (32)5 (33)5 (34)10 (35)5

Page 58, Item 1:
(1)2 (2)4 (3)8 (4)7 (5)8 (6)10 (7)8 (8)5 (9)2
(10)7 (11)3 (12)8 (13)10 (14)2 (15)8 (16)2
(17)6 (18)5 (19)10 (20)2 (21)1 (22)4 (23)4
(24)4 (25)3 (26)9 (27)7 (28)4 (29)3 (30)2
(31)4 (32)3 (33)9 (34)5 (35)8

Page 59, Item 1:
(1)8 (2)8 (3)1 (4)4 (5)2 (6)6 (7)6 (8)7 (9)7
(10)7 (11)7 (12)4 (13)1 (14)6 (15)7 (16)4
(17)8 (18)10 (19)3 (20)8 (21)9 (22)3 (23)5
(24)7 (25)10 (26)7 (27)3 (28)3 (29)10
(30)7 (31)7 (32)6 (33)1 (34)3 (35)3

Page 60, Item 1:
(1)8 (2)3 (3)9 (4)5 (5)10 (6)7 (7)8 (8)3 (9)2
(10)2 (11)10 (12)3 (13)2 (14)10 (15)9
(16)6 (17)6 (18)8 (19)6 (20)1 (21)4 (22)4
(23)4 (24)4 (25)3 (26)6 (27)2 (28)10 (29)3
(30)1 (31)8 (32)9 (33)8 (34)5 (35)3

Page 61, Item 1:
(1)2 (2)8 (3)7 (4)2 (5)6 (6)3 (7)2 (8)4 (9)4
(10)10 (11)9 (12)4 (13)4 (14)3 (15)5 (16)6
(17)10 (18)7 (19)4 (20)5 (21)9 (22)3 (23)3
(24)8 (25)10 (26)4 (27)4 (28)7 (29)2
(30)10 (31)10 (32)8 (33)4 (34)9 (35)10

Page 62, Item 1:
(1)8 (2)7 (3)1 (4)1 (5)8 (6)6 (7)6 (8)1 (9)5
(10)8 (11)2 (12)10 (13)3 (14)6 (15)7 (16)6
(17)5 (18)6 (19)9 (20)2 (21)2 (22)7 (23)7
(24)8 (25)4 (26)3 (27)10 (28)4 (29)7 (30)4
(31)1 (32)1 (33)8 (34)7 (35)6

Page 63, Item 1:
(1)8 (2)9 (3)8 (4)4 (5)5 (6)8 (7)4 (8)10 (9)1
(10)6 (11)5 (12)7 (13)3 (14)10 (15)1 (16)9
(17)4 (18)3 (19)5 (20)6 (21)3 (22)3 (23)8
(24)3 (25)9 (26)5 (27)2 (28)8 (29)10 (30)7
(31)7 (32)8 (33)5 (34)6 (35)4

Page 64, Item 1:
(1)10 (2)10 (3)3 (4)6 (5)4 (6)4 (7)2 (8)3
(9)10 (10)4 (11)1 (12)4 (13)4 (14)4 (15)7
(16)6 (17)5 (18)9 (19)10 (20)9 (21)6 (22)3
(23)1 (24)7 (25)6 (26)1 (27)10 (28)9 (29)5
(30)7 (31)10 (32)8 (33)1 (34)3 (35)8

Page 65, Item 1:
(1)3 (2)7 (3)10 (4)5 (5)10 (6)4 (7)6 (8)8
(9)6 (10)1 (11)2 (12)6 (13)3 (14)9 (15)6
(16)9 (17)7 (18)2 (19)8 (20)7 (21)7 (22)1
(23)3 (24)6 (25)9 (26)1 (27)7 (28)3 (29)7
(30)4 (31)8 (32)4 (33)6 (34)5 (35)2

Page 66, Item 1:
(1)6 (2)1 (3)3 (4)4 (5)7 (6)3 (7)3 (8)8 (9)1
(10)6 (11)10 (12)2 (13)7 (14)3 (15)2 (16)8
(17)4 (18)8 (19)7 (20)1 (21)4 (22)10 (23)5
(24)9 (25)7 (26)8 (27)5 (28)4 (29)1 (30)9
(31)7 (32)9 (33)7 (34)7 (35)8

Page 67, Item 1:
(1)2 (2)1 (3)8 (4)2 (5)5 (6)10 (7)5 (8)10
(9)5 (10)4 (11)9 (12)6 (13)8 (14)6 (15)10
(16)7 (17)4 (18)3 (19)1 (20)3 (21)3 (22)5
(23)7 (24)3 (25)1 (26)5 (27)6 (28)9 (29)2
(30)5 (31)8 (32)6 (33)7 (34)3 (35)5

Page 68, Item 1:
(1)7 (2)10 (3)1 (4)8 (5)4 (6)1 (7)4 (8)1 (9)1
(10)3 (11)1 (12)7 (13)5 (14)2 (15)4 (16)1
(17)1 (18)3 (19)8 (20)1 (21)1 (22)9 (23)3
(24)5 (25)3 (26)3 (27)8 (28)9 (29)8 (30)10
(31)7 (32)3 (33)10 (34)2 (35)8

Page 69, Item 1:
(1)9 (2)4 (3)6 (4)10 (5)6 (6)1 (7)9 (8)3 (9)4
(10)10 (11)1 (12)4 (13)10 (14)4 (15)9
(16)3 (17)3 (18)6 (19)9 (20)4 (21)9 (22)2
(23)3 (24)3 (25)9 (26)9 (27)5 (28)7 (29)6
(30)2 (31)9 (32)5 (33)2 (34)2 (35)3

Page 70, Item 1:
(1)8 (2)5 (3)9 (4)9 (5)4 (6)1 (7)7 (8)10 (9)1
(10)9 (11)7 (12)9 (13)8 (14)10 (15)1
(16)10 (17)7 (18)1 (19)7 (20)10 (21)4
(22)9 (23)3 (24)3 (25)3 (26)8 (27)7 (28)3
(29)4 (30)10 (31)5 (32)9 (33)9 (34)2 (35)6

Page 71, Item 1:
(1)9 (2)3 (3)5 (4)8 (5)7 (6)6 (7)8 (8)2 (9)2
(10)5 (11)8 (12)8 (13)10 (14)10 (15)2
(16)7 (17)8 (18)6 (19)10 (20)2 (21)4
(22)10 (23)5 (24)3 (25)2 (26)9 (27)8 (28)4
(29)6 (30)1 (31)10 (32)1 (33)3 (34)3 (35)4

Page 72, Item 1:
(1)10 (2)9 (3)1 (4)7 (5)3 (6)7 (7)1 (8)6 (9)7
(10)8 (11)8 (12)6 (13)2 (14)8 (15)7 (16)10
(17)9 (18)8 (19)9 (20)2 (21)10 (22)5
(23)10 (24)8 (25)9 (26)10 (27)8 (28)10
(29)10 (30)5 (31)9 (32)5 (33)4 (34)1 (35)6

Page 73, Item 1:
(1)10 (2)8 (3)3 (4)10 (5)5 (6)2 (7)7 (8)9
(9)4 (10)4 (11)7 (12)8 (13)7 (14)6 (15)5

(16)8 (17)7 (18)7 (19)3 (20)8 (21)1 (22)7 (23)2 (24)10 (25)6 (26)7 (27)1 (28)10 (29)10 (30)2 (31)4 (32)9 (33)9 (34)7 (35)6

Page 74, Item 1:
(1)1 (2)6 (3)7 (4)2 (5)10 (6)7 (7)6 (8)10 (9)3 (10)6 (11)5 (12)4 (13)8 (14)6 (15)2 (16)4 (17)5 (18)8 (19)10 (20)1 (21)7 (22)3 (23)1 (24)1 (25)4 (26)10 (27)4 (28)5 (29)4 (30)1 (31)8 (32)2 (33)9 (34)3 (35)8

Page 75, Item 1:
(1)10 (2)7 (3)4 (4)8 (5)8 (6)4 (7)6 (8)3 (9)9 (10)4 (11)6 (12)9 (13)8 (14)10 (15)2 (16)6 (17)8 (18)1 (19)8 (20)5 (21)2 (22)1 (23)4 (24)2 (25)5 (26)2 (27)9 (28)6 (29)6 (30)3 (31)4 (32)2 (33)8 (34)7 (35)1

Page 76, Item 1:
(1)2 (2)8 (3)4 (4)1 (5)10 (6)8 (7)8 (8)3 (9)2 (10)4 (11)8 (12)3 (13)5 (14)3 (15)3 (16)9 (17)8 (18)1 (19)9 (20)9 (21)10 (22)10 (23)8 (24)7 (25)6 (26)10 (27)6 (28)4 (29)1 (30)8 (31)8 (32)1 (33)2 (34)2 (35)9

Page 77, Item 1:
(1)1 (2)2 (3)2 (4)8 (5)1 (6)10 (7)6 (8)9 (9)8 (10)8 (11)1 (12)3 (13)5 (14)7 (15)1 (16)5 (17)1 (18)4 (19)2 (20)6 (21)4 (22)10 (23)6 (24)7 (25)4 (26)8 (27)7 (28)4 (29)10 (30)3 (31)3 (32)3 (33)3 (34)7 (35)7

Page 78, Item 1:
(1)3 (2)6 (3)4 (4)4 (5)10 (6)2 (7)5 (8)1 (9)9 (10)6 (11)3 (12)5 (13)9 (14)4 (15)3 (16)10 (17)7 (18)9 (19)10 (20)1 (21)7 (22)8 (23)3 (24)6 (25)3 (26)7 (27)10 (28)1 (29)8 (30)1 (31)2 (32)7 (33)7 (34)8 (35)7

Page 79, Item 1:
(1)5 (2)1 (3)9 (4)6 (5)4 (6)3 (7)1 (8)4 (9)8 (10)5 (11)1 (12)6 (13)1 (14)7 (15)6 (16)7 (17)4 (18)2 (19)5 (20)3 (21)10 (22)3 (23)5 (24)9 (25)6 (26)4 (27)2 (28)3 (29)8 (30)4

(31)9 (32)1 (33)1 (34)6 (35)3

Page 80, Item 1:
(1)8 (2)6 (3)9 (4)3 (5)9 (6)7 (7)7 (8)7 (9)9 (10)3 (11)6 (12)7 (13)7 (14)5 (15)1 (16)1 (17)1 (18)4 (19)7 (20)2 (21)10 (22)1 (23)3 (24)4 (25)9 (26)1 (27)6 (28)5 (29)4 (30)5 (31)10 (32)2 (33)5 (34)4 (35)3

Page 81, Item 1:
(1)9 (2)4 (3)1 (4)5 (5)9 (6)6 (7)6 (8)8 (9)9 (10)9 (11)10 (12)5 (13)10 (14)9 (15)10 (16)9 (17)7 (18)8 (19)4 (20)6 (21)5 (22)4 (23)8 (24)3 (25)10 (26)1 (27)5 (28)1 (29)7 (30)5 (31)2 (32)6 (33)5 (34)3 (35)1

Page 82, Item 1:
(1)6 (2)1 (3)9 (4)1 (5)8 (6)10 (7)4 (8)6 (9)10 (10)6 (11)2 (12)3 (13)10 (14)10 (15)6 (16)7 (17)1 (18)5 (19)8 (20)4 (21)2 (22)8 (23)6 (24)6 (25)2 (26)5 (27)1 (28)7 (29)5 (30)9 (31)8 (32)9 (33)10 (34)1 (35)8

Page 83, Item 1:
(1)6 (2)3 (3)8 (4)7 (5)3 (6)5 (7)9 (8)1 (9)4 (10)4 (11)4 (12)6 (13)10 (14)2 (15)4 (16)2 (17)8 (18)4 (19)9 (20)6 (21)1 (22)3 (23)8 (24)3 (25)2 (26)4 (27)4 (28)8 (29)6 (30)4 (31)4 (32)8 (33)5 (34)1 (35)4

Page 84, Item 1:
(1)8 (2)7 (3)7 (4)2 (5)7 (6)4 (7)5 (8)5 (9)8 (10)4 (11)6 (12)4 (13)9 (14)4 (15)5 (16)6 (17)5 (18)5 (19)4 (20)7 (21)4 (22)8 (23)4

(24)9 (25)6 (26)7 (27)7 (28)9 (29)3 (30)7
(31)4 (32)4 (33)3 (34)9 (35)1

Page 85, Item 1:
(1)6 (2)6 (3)1 (4)3 (5)8 (6)10 (7)8 (8)3 (9)6
(10)10 (11)3 (12)7 (13)6 (14)2 (15)8
(16)10 (17)7 (18)8 (19)7 (20)3 (21)6 (22)9
(23)9 (24)1 (25)8 (26)3 (27)2 (28)10 (29)1
(30)1 (31)2 (32)3 (33)4 (34)10 (35)10

Page 86, Item 1:
(1)10 (2)6 (3)10 (4)7 (5)3 (6)6 (7)5 (8)3
(9)2 (10)3 (11)7 (12)8 (13)7 (14)2 (15)10
(16)10 (17)4 (18)10 (19)2 (20)1 (21)3
(22)4 (23)4 (24)1 (25)6 (26)5 (27)3 (28)9
(29)10 (30)1 (31)5 (32)2 (33)8 (34)4 (35)9

Page 87, Item 1:
(1)3 (2)9 (3)8 (4)3 (5)7 (6)4 (7)6 (8)7 (9)3
(10)9 (11)9 (12)1 (13)5 (14)4 (15)5 (16)7
(17)4 (18)8 (19)9 (20)7 (21)3 (22)6 (23)6
(24)1 (25)4 (26)2 (27)8 (28)8 (29)6 (30)3
(31)2 (32)4 (33)8 (34)7 (35)5

Page 88, Item 1:
(1)7 (2)7 (3)7 (4)9 (5)9 (6)8 (7)1 (8)3 (9)9
(10)3 (11)3 (12)5 (13)6 (14)1 (15)1 (16)4
(17)5 (18)1 (19)6 (20)2 (21)4 (22)6 (23)1
(24)9 (25)2 (26)4 (27)9 (28)4 (29)4 (30)2
(31)5 (32)2 (33)4 (34)9 (35)9

Page 89, Item 1:
(1)8 (2)6 (3)6 (4)1 (5)5 (6)7 (7)4 (8)8 (9)4
(10)6 (11)2 (12)3 (13)8 (14)7 (15)8 (16)8
(17)2 (18)7 (19)3 (20)3 (21)8 (22)5 (23)8
(24)7 (25)7 (26)2 (27)3 (28)1 (29)1 (30)5
(31)8 (32)6 (33)7 (34)1 (35)6

Page 90, Item 1:
(1)7 (2)6 (3)9 (4)5 (5)6 (6)2 (7)5 (8)4 (9)9
(10)6 (11)4 (12)5 (13)1 (14)7 (15)4 (16)4
(17)2 (18)6 (19)3 (20)4 (21)1 (22)7 (23)4
(24)9 (25)5 (26)6 (27)2 (28)1 (29)3 (30)5
(31)9 (32)1 (33)9 (34)8 (35)9

Page 91, Item 1:
(1)8 (2)3 (3)3 (4)8 (5)9 (6)6 (7)9 (8)3 (9)2
(10)6 (11)9 (12)5 (13)4 (14)5 (15)2 (16)7
(17)1 (18)6 (19)2 (20)6 (21)1 (22)3 (23)7
(24)5 (25)2 (26)5 (27)9 (28)8 (29)6 (30)5
(31)2 (32)4 (33)7 (34)6 (35)7

Page 92, Item 1:
(1)5 (2)9 (3)5 (4)5 (5)4 (6)4 (7)8 (8)3 (9)4
(10)2 (11)4 (12)4 (13)4 (14)7 (15)1 (16)3
(17)2 (18)2 (19)1 (20)2 (21)1 (22)7 (23)6
(24)3 (25)4 (26)8 (27)7 (28)8 (29)4 (30)7
(31)4 (32)4 (33)8 (34)1 (35)6

Page 93, Item 1:
(1)1 (2)2 (3)1 (4)6 (5)2 (6)2 (7)2 (8)6 (9)3
(10)3 (11)4 (12)5 (13)6 (14)9 (15)6 (16)8
(17)6 (18)6 (19)7 (20)8 (21)7 (22)4 (23)7
(24)3 (25)3 (26)9 (27)5 (28)4 (29)1 (30)4
(31)5 (32)2 (33)2 (34)8 (35)4

Page 94, Item 1:
(1)4 (2)5 (3)2 (4)7 (5)3 (6)8 (7)6 (8)5 (9)4
(10)3 (11)4 (12)5 (13)4 (14)2 (15)4 (16)2
(17)6 (18)5 (19)2 (20)9 (21)6 (22)8 (23)4
(24)9 (25)3 (26)7 (27)2 (28)8 (29)3 (30)5
(31)7 (32)4 (33)2 (34)1 (35)6

Page 95, Item 1:
(1)∞ (2)49 (3)9 (4)4 (5)13 (6)3 (7)11 (8)31
(9)7 (10)1 (11)67 (12)19 (13)6 (14)39
(15)53 (16)7 (17)19 (18)42 (19)27 (20)23
(21)79 (22)84 (23)38 (24)37 (25)18 (26)93
(27)79 (28)∞ (29)∞ (30)89 (31)1 (32)5
(33)17 (34)59 (35)35

Page 96, Item 1:
(1)8 (2)99 (3)71 (4)29 (5)41 (6)4 (7)1 (8)∞
(9)28 (10)59 (11)4 (12)∞ (13)94 (14)23
(15)7 (16)89 (17)83 (18)31 (19)13 (20)75
(21)31 (22)∞ (23)1 (24)1 (25)10 (26)31
(27)11 (28)8 (29)17 (30)13 (31)27 (32)3
(33)3 (34)11 (35)72

Page 97, Item 1:
(1)4 (2)47 (3)26 (4)27 (5)17 (6)∞ (7)7 (8)1
(9)51 (10)21 (11)44 (12)19 (13)6 (14)15
(15)3 (16)9 (17)75 (18)74 (19)∞ (20)8
(21)8 (22)67 (23)13 (24)14 (25)7 (26)71
(27)33 (28)22 (29)∞ (30)8 (31)25 (32)43
(33)34 (34)25 (35)11

Page 98, Item 1:
(1)19 (2)23 (3)26 (4)16 (5)17 (6)4 (7)31
(8)29 (9)32 (10)17 (11)1 (12)75 (13)75
(14)6 (15)2 (16)3 (17)19 (18)29 (19)63
(20)52 (21)2 (22)13 (23)86 (24)13 (25)33
(26)78 (27)6 (28)38 (29)85 (30)80 (31)5
(32)29 (33)30 (34)2 (35)9

Page 99, Item 1:
(1)19 (2)16 (3)28 (4)73 (5)96 (6)41 (7)43
(8)7 (9)95 (10)32 (11)5 (12)43 (13)97
(14)9 (15)61 (16)35 (17)83 (18)19 (19)13
(20)3 (21)1 (22)12 (23)38 (24)41 (25)43
(26)58 (27)34 (28)4 (29)13 (30)2 (31)49
(32)29 (33)41 (34)15 (35)17

Page 100, Item 1:
(1)13 (2)1 (3)71 (4)8 (5)47 (6)1 (7)95
(8)26 (9)26 (10)9 (11)74 (12)54 (13)13
(14)24 (15)23 (16)43 (17)5 (18)47 (19)47
(20)1 (21)93 (22)65 (23)13 (24)47 (25)27
(26)41 (27)26 (28)1 (29)9 (30)17 (31)3
(32)79 (33)23 (34)47 (35)2

Leave a Review

Thank you for choosing our math workbook! We value your feedback and would greatly appreciate it if you could take a moment to share your honest review on Amazon.

Your insights will help others make informed decisions and contribute to the improvement of our educational resources.

Thank you for being an essential part of our learning community!

CHECKOUT MORE MATH BOOKS BY ESHAAL MATHS

JUST SCAN THE QR CODE ABOVE!

THANKS!

Made in the USA
Monee, IL
26 November 2024

71330163R00070